MW01593074

Books by

RUSSELL H. CONWELL

OBSERVATION:—EVERY MAN HIS OWN
    UNIVERSITY. Portrait.
ACRES OF DIAMONDS. Illustrated.
WHAT YOU CAN DO WITH YOUR
    WILL POWER

———

HARPER & BROTHERS
[Established 1817]

FOREWORD

PEOPLE are thinking, but they can think much more. The housewife is thinking about the chemical changes caused by heat in meats, vegetables, and liquids. The sailor thinks about the gold in sea-water, the soldier thinks of smokeless powder and muffled guns; the puddler meditates on iron squeezers and electric furnaces; the farmer admires Luther Burbank's magical combinations in plant life; the school-girl examines the composition of her pencil and analyses the writing-paper; the teacher studies psychology at first hand; the preacher understands more of the life that now is; the merchant and manufacturer give more attention to the demand. Yes, we are all thinking. But we are still thinking too far away; even the prism through which we see the stars is near the eyes. The dentist is thinking too much about other people's teeth.

This book is sent out to induce people to look

at their own eyes, to pick up the gold in their laps, to study anatomy under the tutorship of their own hearts. One could accumulate great wisdom and secure fortunes by studying his own finger-nails. This lesson seems the very easiest to learn, and for that reason is the most difficult.

The lecture, "The Silver Crown," which the author has been giving in various forms for fifty years, is herein printed from a stenographic report of one address on this general subject. It will not be found all together, as a lecture, for this book is an attempt to give further suggestion on the many different ways in which the subject has been treated, just as the lecture has varied in its illustrations from time to time. The lecture was addressed to the ear. This truth, which amplifies the lecture, is addressed to the eye.

I have been greatly assisted, and sometimes superseded, in the preparation of these pages by Prof. James F. Willis, of Philadelphia. Bless him!

My hope is by this means to reach a larger audience even than that which has heard some of the things herein so many times in the last forty-five years. We do not hope to give or sell anything to the reader. He has enough already. But many starve with bread in their mouths. They spit it out and weep for food. Humans are

FOREWORD

a strange collection. But they can be induced to think much more accurately and far more efficiently. This book is sent out as an aid to closer observation and more efficient living.

RUSSELL H. CONWELL.

September 1917.

RUSSELL H. CONWELL[1]

AN autobiography! What an absurd request!
If all the conditions were favorable, the
story of my public life could not be made interesting. It does not seem possible that any will
care to read so plain and uneventful a tale.

I was a young man, not yet of age, when I
delivered my first platform lecture. The Civil
War of 1861–65 drew on with all its passions,
patriotism, horrors, and fears, and I was studying
law at Yale University. I had from childhood
felt that I was "called to the ministry." The
earliest event of memory is the prayer of my
father at family prayers in the little old cottage
in the Hampshire highlands of the Berkshire Hills,
calling on God with a sobbing voice to lead me
into some special service for the Saviour. It
filled me with awe, dread, and fear, and I recoiled
from the thought, until I determined to fight

[1]These pages are taken from an autobiographical chapter in
Doctor Conwell's previous book, *Acres of Diamonds*, published
by Harper & Brothers.

against it with all my power. So I sought for other professions and for decent excuses for being anything but a preacher.

Yet while I was nervous and timid before the class in declamation and dreaded to face any kind of an audience, I felt in my soul a strange impulsion toward public speaking which for years made me miserable. The war and the public meetings for recruiting soldiers furnished an outlet for my suppressed sense of duty, and my first lecture was on the "Lessons of History."

That matchless temperance orator and loving friend, John B. Gough, introduced me to the little audience in Westfield, Massachusetts, in 1862. What a foolish little school-boy speech it must have been! But Mr. Gough's kind words of praise, the bouquets, and the applause, made me feel that somehow the way to public oratory would not be so hard as I had feared.

From that time I acted on Mr. Gough's advice and "sought practice" by accepting almost every invitation I received to speak on any kind of a subject.

While I was gaining practice in the first years of platform work, I had the good fortune to have profitable employment as a soldier, or as a correspondent or lawyer, or as an editor, or as a preacher,

which enabled me to pay my own expenses, and
it has been seldom in the fifty years that I have
ever taken a fee for my personal use. In the last
thirty-six years I have dedicated solemnly all the
lecture income to benevolent enterprises. If I
am antiquated enough for an autobiography, perhaps I may be aged enough to avoid the criticism
of being an egotist when I state that some years
I delivered one lecture, "Acres of Diamonds,"
over two hundred times each year, at an average
income of about one hundred and fifty dollars
for each lecture.

Often have I been asked if I did not, in fifty
years of travel in all sorts of conveyances, meet
with accidents. It is a marvel to me that no
such event ever brought me harm. In a con-
tinuous period of over twenty-seven years I delivered about two lectures in every three days,
yet I did not miss a single engagement. Sometimes I had to hire a special train, but I reached
the town on time, with only a rare exception, and
then I was but a few minutes late. Accidents
have preceded and followed me on trains and
boats, and were sometimes in sight, but I was pre-
served without injury through all the years. In
the Johnstown flood region I saw a bridge go out
behind our train. I was once on a derelict steamer

on the Atlantic for twenty-six days. At another time a man was killed in the berth of a sleeper I had left half an hour before. Often have I felt the train leave the track, but no one was killed.

Yet this period of lecturing has been, after all, a side issue. The Temple, and its church, in Philadelphia, which, when its membership was less than three thousand members, for so many years contributed through its membership over sixty thousand dollars a year for the uplift of humanity, have made life a continual surprise; while the Samaritan Hospital's amazing growth, and the Garretson Hospital's dispensaries, have been so continually ministering to the sick and poor, and have done such skilful work for the tens of thousands who ask for their help each year, that I have been happy while away lecturing by the feeling that each hour and minute they were faithfully doing good.

Temple University, which was founded only twenty-seven years ago, has already sent out into a higher income and nobler life nearly a hundred thousand young men and women who could not probably have obtained an education in any other institution. The faithful, self-sacrificing faculty, now numbering two hundred and fifty-three professors, have done the real work. For that I can

INTRODUCTION

claim but little credit; and I mention the university here only to show that my "fifty years on the lecture platform" has necessarily been a side line of work.

My best-known lecture, "Acres of Diamonds," was a mere accidental address, at first given before a reunion of my old comrades of the Forty-sixth Massachusetts Regiment, which served in the Civil War, and in which I was captain. I had no thought of giving the address again, and even after it began to be called for by lecture committees I did not dream that I should live to deliver it, as I now have done, almost five thousand times. "What is the secret of its popularity?" I could never explain to myself or others. I simply know that I always attempt to enthuse myself on each occasion with the idea that it is a special opportunity to do good, and I interest myself in each community and apply the general principles with local illustrations.

RUSSELL H. CONWELL.

SOUTH WORTHINGTON, MASSACHUSETTS,
September 1, 1913.

OBSERVATION:—EVERY MAN HIS OWN UNIVERSITY

OBSERVATION:—EVERY MAN HIS OWN UNIVERSITY

I

OBSERVATION—THE KEY TO SUCCESS

YEARS ago we went up the Ganges River in India. I was then a traveling correspondent, and we visited Argra, the sacred city of northern India, going thence to the Taj Mahal. Then we hired an ox team to take us across country twenty-two miles to visit the summer home of Ackba, the great Mogul of India. That is a wonderful, but dead city.

I have never been sorry that I traversed that country. What I saw and heard furnished me with a story which I have never seen in print. *Harper's Magazine* recently published an illustrated article upon the city, so that if you secure the files you may find the account of that wonderful dead city at Futtepore Sicree.

As we were being shown around those buildings the old guide, full of Eastern lore, told us a tradition connected with the ancient history of that place which has served me often as an illustration of the practical ideas I desire to advance. I wrote it down in the "hen tracks" of shorthand which are now difficult to decipher. But I remember well the story.

He said that there was a beautiful palace on that spot before the great Mogul purchased it. That previous palace was the scene of the traditional story. In the palace there was a throne-room, and at the head of that room there was a raised platform, and upon the platform was placed the throne of burnished gold. Beside the throne was a pedestal upon which rested the wonderful Crown of Silver, which the emperor wore when his word was to be actual law. At other times he was no more than an ordinary citizen. But when he assumed that crown, which was made of silver because silver was then worth much more than gold, his command was as absolute as the law of the Medes and Persians.

The guide said that when the old king who had ruled that country for many years died he was without heirs, leaving no person to claim that throne or to wear that Crown of Silver. The people, believing in the divine right of kings, were unwilling to accept any person to rule who was not born in the royal line. They wasted twelve years in searching for some successor, some relative of the late king. At last the people sank into anarchy, business ceased, famine overspread the land, and the afflicted people called upon the astrologers—their priests—to find a king.

The astrologers, who then worshiped the stars, met in that throne-room and, consulting their curious charts, asked of the stars:

"Where shall we find a successor to our king?"

The stars made to them this reply:

"Look up and down your country, and when you find *a man whom the animals follow, the sun serves, the waters obey, and mankind love*, you need not ask who his ancestors were. This man will be one of the royal line entitled to the throne of gold and the Crown of Silver."

The astrologers dispersed and began to ask of the people:

"Have you seen a man whom the animals follow, the sun serves, the waters obey, and mankind love?"

They were only met with ridicule. At last, in

OBSERVATION:—

his travels, one gray old astrologer found his way into the depths of the Himalaya Mountains. He was overtaken by a December storm and sought shelter in a huntsman's cottage on the side of a mountain.

That night, as he lay awake, weeping for his suffering and dying people, he suddenly heard the howl of a wild beast down the valley. He listened as it drew nearer. He detected "the purr of the hyena, the hiss of the tiger, and the howl of the wolf." In a moment or two those wild animals sniffed at the log walls within which the atrologer lay. In his fright he arose to close the window lest they should leap in where the moonlight entered. While he stood by the window he saw the dark outline of his host, the huntsman, descending the ladder from the loft to the floor. The astrologer saw the huntsman approach the door as though he were about to open it and go out. The astrologer leaped forward, and said:

"Don't open that door! There are tigers, panthers, hyenas, and wolves out there."

The huntsman replied:

"Lie down, my friend, in peace. These are acquaintances of mine."

He flung open the door and in walked tiger, panther, hyena, and wolf. Going to the corner of his hut, the huntsman took down from a cord, stretched across the corner, the dried weeds which he had gathered the fall before because he *had noticed* that those weeds were antidotes for poisoned wild animals. Those poisoned animals had sniffed the antidote from afar and gathered at his door. When he opened that door they followed him to the corner of the hut, in peace with one another because of their common distress. He fed each one the antidote for which it came, and each one licked his hand with thanks and turned harmlessly out the door. Then the huntsman closed the door after the last one, and went to his rest as though nothing remarkable had happened.

This is the fabulous tradition as it was told me. When the old astrologer lay down on his rug after the animals were gone, he said to himself, "The animals follow him," and then he caught upon the message of the stars and said, "It may be this huntsman is the king," but on second thought he said, "Oh no; he is not a king. How would he look on a throne of gold and wearing a Crown of Silver—that ignorant, horny-handed man of the mountains? He is not the king."

The next morning it was cold and they desired a fire, and the huntsman went outside and gathered some leaves and sticks. He put them in the center of the hut upon the ground floor. He then drew aside a curtain which hid a crystal set in the roof, which he had placed there because he *had noticed* that the crystal brought the sunlight to a focused point upon the floor. Then the astrologer saw, as that spot of light approached the leaves and sticks with the rising of the sun, the sticks began to crackle. Then the leaves began to curl, little spirals of smoke arose, and a flame flashed forth. As the astrologer looked on that rising flame, he said to himself:

"The sun has lit his fire! The sun serves him; and the animals followed him last night; after all, it may be that he is the king.

But on second thought he said to himself again: "Oh, he is not the king; for how would I look with all my inherited nobility, with all my wealth, cultivation, and education, as an ordinary citizen of a kingdom of which this ignorant fellow was a king? It is far more likely to be me."

A little later the astrologer desired water to drink, and he applied to the huntsman, and the huntsman said, "There is a spring down in the valley where I drink."

So down to the spring went the astrologer. But the wind swept down and roiled the shallow water so that he could not drink, and he went back and complained of that muddy water. The huntsman said:

"Is that spring rebellious? I will teach it a lesson."

Going to another corner of his hut, he took down a vial of oil which he himself had collected, and, going down to the spring with the vial of oil, he dropped the oil upon the waters. Of course, the surface of the spring became placid beauty. As the astrologer dipped his glittering bowl into the flashing stream and partook of its cooling draught, he felt within him the testimony, "This is the king, for the waters obey him!" But again he hesitated and said, "I hope he is not the king."

The next day they went up into the mountains, and there was a dam holding back, up a valley, a great reservoir of water. The astrologer said, "Why is there a dam here with no mill?" And the huntsman said: "A few years ago I was down on the plains, and the people were dying for want of water. My heart's sympathies went out for the suffering and dying humanity, and when I came back here *I noticed* . . ."

I may as well stop here in this story and emphasize this phrase. He said, "When I came back here *I noticed*." This is the infallible secret

7

of success. I wish you to be happy; I wish you to be mighty forces of God and man; I wish you to have fine homes and fine libraries and money invested, and here is the only open road to them. By this road only have men who have won great success traveled.

The huntsman said: "When I came back here *I noticed* a boulder hanging on the side of the mountain. *I noticed* it could be easily dislodged, and *I noticed* that it would form an excellent anchorage in the narrow valley for a dam. *I noticed* that a small dam here would hold back a large body of water in the mountain. I let the boulder fall, filled in for the dam, and gathered the water. Now every hot summer's day I come out and dig away a little more of the dam, and thus keep the water running in the river through the hot season. Then, when the fall comes on, I fill up the dam again and gather the waters for the next year's supply."

When the astrologer heard that he turned to the huntsman and said:

"Do mankind down on the plains know that you are their benefactor?"

"Oh yes," said he; "they found it out. I was down there a little while ago, selling the skins I had taken in the winter, and they came around me, kissed me, embraced me, and fairly mobbed me with their demonstrations of gratitude. I will never go down on the plains again."

When the astrologer heard that *mankind loved him,* all four conditions were filled. He fell upon his knees, took the horny hand of the huntsman, looked up into his scarred face, and said:

"Thou art a king born in the royal line. The stars did tell us that when we found a man whom the animals followed, the sun served, the waters obeyed, and mankind loved, he would be the heir entitled to the throne, and thou art the man!"

But the huntsman said: "I a king! Oh, I am not a king! My grandfather was a farmer!"

The astrologer said: "Don't talk about your grandfather. That has nothing to do with it. The stars told us thou art the man."

The huntsman replied: "How could I rule a nation, knowing nothing about law? I never studied law!"

Then the astrologer cut short the whole discussion with a theological dictum quoted from the ancient sacred books, which I will give in a very literal translation:

"Let not him whom the stars ordain to rule dare disobey their divine decree."

OBSERVATION:—

Now I will put that into a phrase a little more modern:

"Never refuse a nomination!"

When the huntsman heard that very wise decision he consented to be led down to the Juna Valley and to the beautiful palace. There they clothed him in purple. Then, amid the acclaim of happy and hopeful people, they placed upon his brow that badge of kingly authority—the Silver Crown. For forty years after that, so the old guide said to us, he ruled the nation and brought it to a peace and prosperity such as it had never known before and has never enjoyed since.

That wonderful tradition, so full of illustrative force, has remained with me all the subsequent years. When I look for a man to do any great work, I seek one having these four characteristics. If he has not all four he must have some of them, or else he is good for little in modern civilization.

II

WHO THE REAL LEADERS ARE

AMONG all of you who read this book I am looking for the kings and queens. I am looking for the successful men and women of the future. No matter how old you may be, you yet have life before you. I am looking for the leading men and women, and I will find them with these four tests. I cannot fail; it is infallible.

Some men, intensely American, will say:

"Oh, we don't have any kings or queens in this country."

Did you ever observe that America is ruled by the least number of people of any nation known on earth? And that same small number will rule it when we add all the women, as we soon shall, to the voting population. America is ruled by a very few kings and queens. The reason why we are ruled by so few is because our people are generally intelligent. "Oh," you will ask, "do you mean the political boss rule?" Yes. That is not a good word to use, because it is misleading. America is ruled by bosses, anyhow, and it will be so long as we are a free people. We do not approve of certain phases of boss rule, and so don't misunderstand me when I state that a very few persons govern the American people. In my home city, Philadelphia, for instance, nearly two millions of people are ruled by four or five men. It will always be so. Everything depends on whether those four or five men are fitted for the place of leaders or not. If they are wise men and good men, then that is the best kind of government. There is no doubt about it. If all the eighty or ninety millions of people in the United States were compelled to vote on every little thing that was done by the Government, you would be a long time getting around to any reform.

An intelligent farmer would build a house. Will he, as a farmer, go to work and cut out that lumber himself, plane it himself, shape it himself? Will he be the architect of the house, drive all the nails, put on the shingles, and build the chimney himself? If he is an intelligent man he will hire a carpenter, an architect, and a mason who understand their business, and tell them to oversee that work for him. In an intelligent country we can hire men who understand statesmanship, law, social economics, who love justice. We hire them as skilled people to do what we are not able to do. Why should all the people be all the time meddling with something they don't understand? They employ people who do understand it, and consequently, in a free nation a few specially fitted people will ever be allowed to guide. They will be the people who know better than we know what to do under difficult or important circumstances.

You are ruled by a few people, and I am looking for these few people among my readers. There are some women in this country who now have more influence than any known statesman, and their names are hardly mentioned in the newspapers. I remember once, in the days of Queen Victoria, asking a college class, "Who rules England?" Of course, they said, "Queen Victoria." Did Queen Victoria rule England? During her nominal reign England was the freest land on the face of the earth, and America not half as free if you go to the extremes of comparison. She was only a figurehead, and she would not even express an opinion on the Boer War. It was all left to the statesmen, who had really been selected by the Parliament to rule. They were the real rulers.

OBSERVATION:—

I am looking for the real kings, not the nominal ones, and I shall find the successful men and women of the future by the four tests mentioned in the old tradition of the Silver Crown. The first one is:

"Animals will follow them."

If a dog or cat tags your heels to-morrow remember what I am writing about it here. It is evidence of kingship or queenship. If you don't have a cat or dog or an ox or a horse to love you, then I pity you. I pity the animal the most, but you are also a subject of sympathy. Is there no lower animal that loves to hear your footstep, whines after your heels, or wags the tail or shakes the head at your door? Is there no cat that loves to see you come in when the house has been vacant? Is there no faithful dog that rises and barks with joy when he hears your key in the door? If you have none it is time you had one, because one of the important pathways to great success is along the line of what animal life can give to us of instruction and encouragement.

The time has come when a dog ought to be worth at least a thousand dollars. The time has come when a horse that now trots a mile in 2:05 or 2:06 ought to trot a mile in fifty-five seconds. That is scientifically possible. Now, where are your deacons and your elders and your class leaders that you haven't a horse in your city that will trot a mile in fifty-five seconds?

"Oh," says some good, pious brother, "I don't pay any attention to trotting-horses! I am too religious to spend time over them."

Is that so? Who made the trotting-horse? Who used the most picturesque language on the face of the earth, in the Book of Job, to describe him? Did you ever own a trotting-horse? Did you ever see a beautiful animal so well fed, so well cared for, trembling on that line with his mane shaking, his eyes flashing, his nostrils distended, and all his being alert for the leap? And did you hear the shot and see him go? If you did and didn't love him, you ought to be turned out of the church.

The time has come when a horse may be as useful as a university.

At Yale University, one day, I heard a professor of science tell those boys that a horse has within its body so much galvanic or electric force continually generated by the activities of life, that if that electricity could be concentrated and held to a certain point, a horse could stand still and run a forty-horse power electric engine. He went further than that and said that a man has within his living body sufficient continually generated electricity which, if it were brought to a point, might enbable him to stand still and run a ten-horsepower electric engine. I went out of that class-room with a sense of triumph, thinking:

"There is going to be use, after all, for the loafers who stand on the corners and smoke!"

In Europe, some years ago, a sewing-machine was invented on which a lady put her bare feet, and her electric forces started the machine. This power does not yet run the machine strong enough to force the needle for real sewing. The only question is to get more of the electricity of that lady through the machine and secure the greater power. Then if a young man wants a valuable wife he must marry one "full of lightning."

The time is very near at hand when all the motive power of the world may be furnished by animal life. When they get one step further the greatest airships will go up and take with them a lap dog. The airship will require no coal, no oil, but just the electric force of that lap dog; and if they carry up enough to feed that dog he will furnish the power to run the motors. The great high seas of the air will be filled with machines run by lap dogs or the electricity of the aviator himself. It is not so far away as many of you may suppose, and it is the greatly needed improvement of this time, not so much for the purpose of the war, as for peace.

The time has come when an old hen may become a great instructor of the world. I would rather send my child to an old hen than to any professor I ever saw in my life. That old biddy which scratches around your door, or who cackles beside your fence, or picks off your flowers, knows more of some things than any scientific professor on the face of the earth. I wish I knew what that old hen does. But there are some professors who pretend to have a wonderful intellect, who say:

"I graduated from Leipsic or from Oxford or Harvard, and I have no time to observe a hen."

No time to notice a hen? My friend, did you ever try to talk with her?

"No, I did not; she has no language."

Didn't you ever hear her call the chickens and see them come? Didn't you ever hear her scold the rooster, and see him go? Well, a hen does have a real language, and it is time you scientific professors understood what that old biddy says.

"Oh, but," says the professor, "I have no time to spend with a hen! They are around the place all the time, but I never take any special notice of them. I am studying the greater things in the world."

"Won't you come into my study a minute, professor, and let me examine you? You have examined the boys long enough, now let me examine you."

Bring all you know of science and all the scientific applications ever made, and all the instruments that are ever used, bring all that the world has ever discovered of chemistry. Come, and take in your hand a dove's egg, just the egg. Now, professor, will you tell the person who is reading this book where, in this egg, is now the beating heart of the future bird? Can you tell where it is?

"Oh no, I cannot tell that. I can tell you the chemistry of the egg."

"No, I am not looking for that. I am looking for the design in the egg. I am looking for something more divinely mysterious than anything of chemistry. Now, professor, will you tell me where in that egg is the bony frame that next will appear?"

"No, I cannot tell you that."

"Where is the sheening bosom, and where the wings that shall welcome the sun in its coming?"

"No man can tell that," says the professor.

EVERY MAN HIS OWN UNIVERSITY

The professor is quite right. It cannot yet be told. Yet, in that egg is the greatest scientific problem with which the world has ever grappled— the beginning of life and the God-given design. In that egg is the secret of life. Professor, tell me where this life begins. The professor says, "No man can answer questions like that."

Then, until we can answer, we must take off our hats every time we meet a setting hen. For that old biddy knows by instinct more about it than any one of us. She knows directly, through her instinctive nature from God, something about the beginnings of life that we cannot understand yet.

The last time I saw Dr. Oliver Wendell Holmes, the grand poet of Massachusetts, he asked me to go out in his back yard and see his chickens. He told me they would answer to their names. But it turned out that they were like our children, and would not show off before company. But I haven't any doubt those little chickens still with the hen did answer to their individual names when she alone called them. I am sure that great man understood the hen and chickens as fully as Darwin did the doves.

It was a wonderful thing for science that men like Holmes and Darwin could learn so much from the hen. It reminds me of a current event in Doctor Holmes's own life, though the biographies do not seem to have taken notice of it. He and Mr. Longfellow were very intimate friends. They were ever joking each other like two boys, always at play whenever they met. One day, it is said, Doctor Holmes asked Mr. Longfellow to go down to Bridgewater, in Massachusetts, to a poultry show. He went; he was greatly interested in chickens.

Those two great poets went down to the poultry show, and as they walked up the middle passageway between the exhibits of hens and chickens they came to a large poster on which was a picture of a rooster. He had his wings spread and mouth open, making a speech to a lot of little chickens. It was such a unique picture that Mr. Longfellow called Doctor Holmes's attention to it, and said:

"There, you love chickens, you understand them. What do you suppose a rooster does say when he makes a speech to chickens like that?"

They went on, and Doctor Holmes was studying over it. Finally he turned around and said, "Go on, I will catch up with you." He went back to that poster, got up on a chair, took the tacks out of the top, turned in the advertisement at the top, above the picture, and then took his pencil and drew a line from the bill of the rooster that was making that speech up to the top. There he wrote what he thought that rooster was saying to those chickens. They say that he did not make a single correction in it, of line or word. He then went after Mr. Longfellow and brought the great poet back to see the poster. He had written these words, in imitation of Longfellow's "Psalm of Life":

Life is real, life is earnest!
  And the shell is not its pen;
Egg thou art, and egg remainest,
  Was not spoken of the hen,

Art is long, and Time is fleeting,
  Be our bills then sharpened well,
And not like muffled drums be beating,
  On the inside of the shell.

In the world's broad field of battle,
  In the great barnyard of life,
Be not like those lazy cattle!
  Be a rooster in the strife!

Lives of roosters all remind us,
  We can make our lives sublime,
And when roasted, leave behind us
  Hen tracks on the sands of time.

OBSERVATION:—

Hen tracks that perhaps another
Chicken drooping in the rain,
Some forlorn and hen-pecked brother,
When he sees, shall crow again.

Animal life can do much for us if we will but
study it, take notice of it daily in our homes, in
the streets, wherever we are.

III

MASTERING NATURAL FORCES

IT has been demonstrated by science that the mentality and disposition of all kinds of animal life are greatly affected by what they eat. Professor Virchow, of Germany, took two little kittens and fed them on different foods, but kept them in the same environment. After three months he went in and put out his finger at one of those little kittens, and it stuck up its back and spit and scratched and drew the blood. It was savage. He put out his finger to the other kitten, fed on the other food, and it rubbed against his finger and purred with all the loveliness of domestic peace. What was the difference between the kittens? Nothing in the world but what they ate.

Now I can understand why some men swear and some women scratch. It is what they eat.

The universities of the world are now establishing schools of domestic science for the purpose

23

EVERY MAN HIS OWN UNIVERSITY

But I will not follow this thought into the thousands of discoveries animals suggest, because, in this wonderful tradition, the real king was not only followed by animals, but "the sun served him, and the waters obeyed him." Now I can combine those two thoughts for illustration, using the wonderful locomotive which draws our railway trains. The locomotive has within it the coal, which is the carbon of the sun. Thus the sun serves man by heating the water; and there is the water changing to steam and driving the piston-rods over the land, obeying man.

We need so much to travel faster than we do now. I saw a man not long ago who said he did not like to travel a mile a minute in a railway train. If you don't go faster than a mile a minute ten years from now you will feel like that old lady who got in a slow train with a little girl. The conductor came through and asked for a ticket for the little girl, and the old lady said:

"She is too young to pay her fare."

"No," said the conductor. "A great girl like that must pay her fare."

"Well," the mother replied, "she was young enough to go for nothing when we got in this train."

You will feel like that if you don't travel faster

than a mile a minute ten years from now. The time is soon coming when, in order to go from Philadelphia to San Francisco, you will get in the end of a pipe or on a wire, and about as quick as you can say "that" you will be in San Francisco. Is that an extravagant expression? The time draws nigh when you won't say that is an extravagant expression. As I am writing this a company to lay that long-contemplated pneumatic tube from New York to Boston is being formed. They have been fighting in the courts over the right to lay it. When they finish it you can put a hundredweight of goods in the New York end of it, and it will possibly land in Boston in one minute and fifty-eight seconds. Now, then, what is to hinder making a little larger pipe and putting a man in and sending him in one minute and fifty-eight seconds? The only reason why you cannot send them with that lightning speed is for the same reason, perhaps, that the Irishman gave when he fell from a tall building and they asked, "Didn't the fall hurt you?" "No, it was not the falling that hurt me, it was the stopping so quick." That is all the difficulty there is in using now those pneumatic tubes for human travel.

We need those inventions now. We are soon

going to find the inventors. Will you find them graduating from some university, or from some great scientific school at Harvard, Yale, Oxford, or Berlin? It may be. I would not say, while presiding over a university myself, that you would not find such people there. Perhaps you will.

But come back in history with me a little way and let us see where these men and women are to be found. Go into northern England, and go down a coal shaft underground two miles, and there is a young man picking away at a vein of coal a foot and a half thick. His hair sticks out through his hat, his face is besmirched, his fingers are covered with soot. Yet he is digging away and whistling. Is he a king? One of the greatest the world has ever seen. Queen Victoria, introducing her son, who has since been king, to that young man, said to him:

"I introduce you, my son, to England's greatest man."

What! This poor miner, who has never been to school but a few months in his life? While he had not been to a day school, he had been learning all the time in the university of experience, in the world's great university—*every-day observation*. When such a man graduates he gets the highest possible degree—D.N.R.—"Don't Need Recommends." Let us go in the mine and ask the miner his name.

"Young man, what is your name?"

"Stevenson."

The inventor of the locomotive itself! Oh, where are thy kings, oh, men? They may be in the mine, on the mountain, in the hovel or the palace, wherever a man notices what other people have not seen. Wherever a man observes in his every-day work what other people have not noticed, there will be found the king.

Are any of my readers milkmen? Are you discouraged when the brooks freeze up in the winter? Now, there was a milkman in West Virginia, not many years ago, who went to the train every morning with the milk from the farm, and while they were putting the milk in the car he studied the locomotive standing in the station.

"What do you know about a locomotive?"

"Oh, I don't know anything about it."

Is that so? You have seen and ridden after them all your lifetime, and you have seen them standing in the station, you have looked at the immense structure with some respect, but you don't know anything about it—and then you expect to be a successful man! That young man became interested in the locomotive, and while he stood around there he watched it, measured it, asked the engineer questions about it. One day the engineer, seeing he was interested, took him down to the switch and showed him how to put on the steam, and how to shut it off, and how to reverse the engine, ring the bell, operate the whistle, and all about it, and he was delighted. He went home and made draftings in the evenings of the locomotive.

Two years after that the same train ran on the siding and the engineer and fireman went into a house to get their breakfast, leaving the locomotive alone—waiting for the snow to be shoveled off the track which had rolled down the mountain. While they were absent a valve of the engine accidentally opened. It started the piston, and the engine began to draw out the train on to the main track, and then it began to go down the fearful grade at full speed. The brakeman went out on the rear platform, caught hold of the wheel brake in order to slow down the train. When he saw the engineer and fireman at the top of the hill swinging their arms as though something awful had happened, the brakeman shouted:

"There is the engineer and fireman, both of them, up there. We will all be killed!"

OBSERVATION:—

The people fainted and screamed, and the cry went to the second car, and then to the baggage car, and that milkman was there. He ran to the side-door to leap, but saw that it would be certain death. Then, with the help of the baggage-man he clambered over the tender, reached the engineer's place, and felt around for the lever in the smoke. When he discovered it he pressed it home. Then reversed the engine. It was a wonder those cylinder heads held. But with an awful crack the driving wheels stopped on the track, shot fire through the snow as they began to roll back against the ongoing train, the momentum still pushing it on. It shook the train until every pane of glass was broken. When it came to a stop the passengers climbed out to ascertain who stopped the train. They discovered that this young man had done it, and saved their lives, and they thanked him with tears.

A stockholder in the railroad company, an old man nearly eighty years of age, was on the train. He went into the stockholders' meeting that night and told the story of his narrow escape on that train. Since then that milkman has been one of the richest railroad owners in the world.

What do you suppose has become of the other milkmen who went at the same time to the same

30

place and sat on the edge of the platform and swung their feet? What has become of them?

Ask the winds that sweep down from the Alleghany mountains—where are the other milk-men? The winds will answer, "They are going to the pump there still."

It was ever the same. Wherever you look, success in any branch of achievement depends upon this ability to get one's education every day as one goes along from the events that are around us now. The king is found wherever a person notices that which other men do not see.

3

IV

WHOM MANKIND SHALL LOVE

THE great scientific men—and we need more—often are not given the full credit that is due them because they have not "graduated" from somewhere. It seems to me there is a feeling in these later days for creating an aristocracy among the men who have graduated from some rich university. But that does not determine a man's life. It may be a foolish tyranny for a little while, but nevertheless every man and woman must finally take the place where he and she are best fitted to be, and do the things that he and she can do best, and the things about which he and she really know. Where they graduated, or when, will not long count in the race of practical life.

We need great scientific men now more than we ever needed them before. Where are you going to find them? We won't find them where that scientific man came from who invented an improvement upon the cuckoo clock. His clock, instead of saying, "Cuckoo, cuckoo, cuckoo," when it struck the hour, said, "I love you! I love you! I love you!" That man left the clock at home with his wife nights while he was around at the club, thinking that would be sufficient protestation of his love. Yet any man knows you cannot make love by machinery. That was only a so-called scientific idea.

I read not long ago that a great scientific man said that "love and worship are only the aggregate results of physical causes." That is not true. Love and worship are something beyond physical causes. Educated men ought to know better than to say anything like that.

There are many valuable things that every man knows until he has unlearned them in a university.

There is danger that a man will get so much education that he won't know anything of real value because his useless education has driven the useful out of his mind. It is like a dog I owned when a boy. He was a very good fox dog. One day I thought I would show him off before the boys. We let the fox out at the barn door, which was open just far enough for the dog to see the fox start. Then he began whining and yelping to get out. I ran out and dropped some red pepper where the dog was likely to follow the fox over the hill. Then I went back and opened the door. The dog rushed out after the fox, but soon began to take in the red pepper. Then he began to whine and yelp—and stopped, whirled around, and, rushing down to the brook, put his nose under the water. From the time he graduated from that pepper university he never would follow a fox at all. He had added education in the wrong direction, and so it is often with these scientific men.

Do you know that the humblest man, whatever his occupation, really knows instinctively certain things better for not having been to school much? It is so easy to bias the mind.

When the boy comes to learn geometry the teacher will say: "Two parallel lines will never run together." The boy may look up and ask, "What is the use of telling me that?" Every man knows that two parallel lines will never run together. But how does he know it? It is born with him. His natural instincts tell that to him. It is what we call "an axiom"—a self-evident truth. It is above argument and beyond all possible reasoning. We know that "two halves are equal to the whole"! You know that when you cut an apple in half the two halves are equal to the whole of it. You tell that to a geometry class, and they say: "I know that. Everybody knows it." Of course everybody does, because it is a natural scientific fact that you cannot reasonably question.

Ask a man, "Do you know that you exist?" He looks with astonishment and says: "Certainly! Don't I know that I am? I know that I am here, that this is me, that I am not Mrs. Smith or some one else?"

Of course you do. But how do you know it? By a God-given instinct that came into the world with you.

No scientist or school on earth could disprove that, or prove it, either. It is a self-evident fact. I know that I am an intelligent personal identity, and that I dwell in this body in some mysterious way. I know that is my hand, but what I possess is not me. I know by an instinct infallible that I am a spiritual being, separate from this material. You know that. No scientist can prove or disprove it. It is a fact we all know. I know that I can never die, and you know it unless you have gotten educated out of it. It is in your very life; it is a part of your original instinct.

OBSERVATION:—

When some graduate of some great university shall come to you, young man, and say, "I can prove to you that the Bible is not true," or, "I can prove to you that your religion is false," you can say to him: "You are nothing but an educated fool. Because the more you have studied the less truth you seem to know."

It is only one's own personal self that can know his own religious instincts. It is only himself that can know whether he is in spiritual relation to God or not. No education on earth can overturn the fact, although wrong study may confuse the mind.

When a man comes to me, with his higher education, to overturn religion, it reminds me of what Artemus Ward said to that lordly graduate of Oxford and Cambridge. This man told Ward that he was disgusted with his shows. Artemus Ward asked him, "What do you know about these shows?" and he said: "I know everything about them. I graduated from two universities." Then Artemus Ward said, "You remind me of a farmer in Maine who had a calf that stole the milk of two cows, and the more milk he got the greater calf he was." Such is the effect sometimes of education on religious life—the more mental education of some kind which you get the less you may know about your natural religious instincts.

There is a great need to-day, and prayers go up to heaven now for men and women whom *mankind shall love*—love because they are great benefactors; love because, while they are making money or gaining fame or honor for themselves, they are blessing humanity all the way along. I must not argue now. I will illustrate, because you can remember the illustrations and you might forget an argument.

There is a great need for artists. There never was such a need in the progress of Christian civilization as there is now for great painters. All these walls ought to be covered with magnificent paintings teaching some great divine truth, and every school-house, yes, every barn, ought to have some picture upon it that will instruct and inspire. All our children seek to go to the moving pictures, and that shows what an agency there is in pictures for the instruction of mankind. We need artists by the thousands. It is not a surprise to me that a New York man is getting a salary of $35,000 a year for moving-picture work because "he notices something other people have not seen." It is no surprise that a great store in that city pays an advertising man $21,000 a year salary. He can see what the rest of the public does not see.

We need great artists, hundreds of them. Where are you going to find them? You will say "at the art school, in the National Gallery in London, or at the Louvre in Paris, or in Rome." Well, it may be that you will. But it is an unfortunate thing for your theory that one of the greatest painters in America painted with a cat's tail. It is another enlightening thing that the man who received the highest prize at the World's Fair in Chicago for a landscape painting never took "a lesson" in color or drawing in his life.

But that doesn't argue against lessons nor against schools or universities. Don't misunderstand me in this. I am only making emphatic my special subject.

He took the highest prize and never went to an art school in his life. If he had attended school the teacher might have tried to show him something and thus weakened his mind. The teacher in a school who shows a child anything that that child could work out for himself is a curse to that child. It is an awful calamity for a child to be under the control of a too kind-hearted teacher who will show him everything.

One of the greatest artists was Charlotte

Brontë. She was a wonderful little woman, and I like little women. Did you ever read Longfellow's poem on "Little Women"? It always reminds me so much of Charlotte Brontë. One day he showed me the poem, and I asked him why he did not print it in his book, and he replied, "I don't think it is worth while." Since his death they have given it first rank, and I will quote one verse:

As within a little rose we find the richest dyes,
As in a little grain of gold much price and value lies,
And as from a little balsam much odor doth arise,
So in a little woman there's a gleam of paradise.

Charlotte Brontë was one of those wonderful, wiry, beautiful little cultivated combinations of divine femininity which no man can describe. She had a younger brother on her hands, and when a young woman has a younger brother on her hands if she has a beau, she has her hands full. This younger brother was dull of brains, clumsy of finger and unfitted to be an artist. But his sister was determined he should be a painter, and took him to the shore, to the village and the woods, and said, "Notice everything, and notice it closely." Finally, he did secure a second prize. Then his little sister threw her arms about her brother's neck and kissed him, and thanked him for getting that prize. That is just like a woman! I never could understand a woman. Of all the mysterious things that the Lord ever put together, a woman is the most mysterious. Charlotte Brontë was like an old lady I used to know up in my native town who thanked her husband, with tears, for having brought up a flock of sheep which she herself fed every morning through the winter before he was out of bed.

Finally, Charlotte Brontë's younger brother became dissipated and died, and then her father died, and when we ministers get to be old we might as well die. She was left without means of support. But when she told her friends, they said "You have a college education, Charlotte. Why don't you write something?" We now find that the first thing she wrote was " Jane Eyre," the wonderful story for which she at last received $38,000. Queen Victoria invited that humble girl to her palace at Windsor because of her marvelous genius.

How came she to write a book like that? Simply because she had noticed so closely, for her brother's sake, that from the nib of her pen flowed those beautiful descriptions as naturally as the water ripples down the mountain-side. That is always so. No man ever gives himself for others' good in the right spirit without receiving "a hundredfold more in this present time."

I will go one step farther with this thought. We do need great painters, but we don't want more painters like that man who painted the Israelites coming out of Egypt, representing them with muskets on their shoulders with U. S. on the butts.

But more than artists we need great musicians. There is an awful need of music. We have too much noise, but very little real music. Did you ever think how little you have? Do you suppose a true musician is simply a man who roars down to low B and squeals to high C? What an awful need there is of the music which refines the heart, brightens the mind; that brings glory and heaven down to men. I have not the space here to expand upon that thought—the awful need of humanity for real music. But we don't get it. I do not know why it is. I am not able to explain. But perhaps I can hint at what music is.

At Yale I had to earn my own living, and that is why, for these forty-four years, I have been lecturing exclusively to help young men secure their college education. I arose at four o'clock and worked in the New Haven House from four to

eight to get the "come backs" from the breakfast table so that my brother and I could live.
Some days, however, I digged potatoes in the
afternoon, and taught music in the evening,
although the former was my proper occupation.
Sometimes my music scholars would invite me
in to play something to entertain their company,
and I noticed the louder I played the louder they
talked. I often said, "What a low standard of
musical culture there is in New Haven! But I
learned something after I left college. I learned
I was not a musician.

Had I been a musician they would have listened. That is the only test of real music. There
is no other.

If you sing and every one whispers, or you play
and every one talks, it is because you are not a
musician. I dare tell it to you here, when I would
not dare say it to you individually if we were
alone. There is no person on earth who gets so
many lies to the square inch as a person who drums
on a piano.

What is music? Music may be wholly a personal
matter and be called music. I remember Major
Snow, of my native town, who used to listen to the
filing of the saw at the sawmill. How that did
screech and scratch until it hurt to our toes!

EVERY MAN HIS OWN UNIVERSITY

We asked the old major why he went down to the mill Saturday, when he could go any other day. He said: "Oh, boys, you do not understand it. When I was young I worked in a sawmill and I come down here to hear them file that saw. It reminds me of the good old days. It is music to me." He was "educated up" to that standard where filing of a saw was music to him, and so men may be educated in all manner of ways in so-called music. But it is not the real music.

What is true music? I went to a beautiful church in New York to exchange with the pastor, and an officer of the church came down the aisle as I walked in and said to me, "Sir, the choir always opens the service." They did; they opened it! I sat down on the pulpit sofa and waited an embarrassingly long time for something to be done up there. The choir roosted on a shelf over my head. The soprano earned $4,000 a year, and I was anxious to hear her. Soon I heard the rustle of silk up there, and one or two little giggles. Then the soprano began. She struck the lowest note her cultivated voice could possibly touch, and then she began to wind, or rather, cork-screw, her way up and up and up, out of sight— and she stayed up there. Then the second bass began and wound his way down, down, down—

down to the Hades of sound—and he stayed down there.

Now, was that music? Was it worship? Why, if I had stood in that sacred place and positively sworn at the people it would not have been greater sacrilege than that exhibition up on that shelf! Do you think the living God is to be worshiped by a high-flying, pyrotechnic, trapeze performance in acoustics? Neither worship nor music was there. Music does not consist of a high-flying circus trapeze performance in acoustics.

What is music? Music is such a combination of sound as moves the heart to holier emotions, quickens the brain to brighter thoughts, and moves the whole man on to nobler deeds. That is music. Nothing else is music. You can only find out whether you are a musician or not by *taking notice*, while you sing, whether you hold the attention of the people, and whether you influence their memory and their after character.

EVERY MAN HIS OWN UNIVERSITY

V

NEED OF ORATORS

WE need great orators. The need is something alarming. I am often called to lecture at the Chautauquas and the lyceums, and the committees often urge me to recommend some man or woman who will fill a place on the public platform. They offer marvelous rewards for those who will do that well. There are no men or women alive, not one known in our land to-day, who could be called a great orator. When I began to lecture, fifty-eight years ago, there were Henry Ward Beecher, Wendell Phillips, George William Curtis, Edward Everett, the greatest orator of his day—and John B. Gough. I esteem it a great honor to have been induced by Mr. Gough to go on the lecture platform. They are all gone, and no successors have appeared.

Liberty and oratory have ever gone together, and always will, hence the need of oratory is especially pressing now.

OBSERVATION:—

Why don't we have orators? The editors say "because the newspaper has come in and goes into every home, and a man on Sunday will read a better sermon in his newspaper than ever was delivered, and will save paying the minister and having trouble with the choir." Now, that time will never come. You will never get along without real orators, no matter how many newspapers you may have. I respect the press. I have had something to do with its work in my lifetime. I have worked upon and owned a daily newspaper. But I must say that there is something, after all, in the shake of a living man's finger, something in the flash of his eye, something in the stamp of his foot, but vastly more in his mesmeric power, which no cold type will ever express! You never can fully express the living man in cold lead.

Why don't we have great orators? I don't think the newspapers are in the way. But other people say to me. "It is the injurious effect of the modern school of elocution, which is now called 'the school of oratory.'" It has only been a few years since all these elocutionary schools changed their names to "schools of oratory" and consequently damaged the prospect of our country. The school of elocution may not be a school of oratory at all. It may be a hindrance to oratory;

it depends on what the teaching is. There is a wide difference between elocution and real oratory. Elocution is an art of expression, which every teacher has, and he teaches his own art. But oratory is the great science of successful speech. The man who gets what he pleads for is an orator, no matter how he calls. If you call a dog and he comes, that is oratory. If he runs away, that is elocution!

Why don't we have greater orators? These schools of elocution remind me of an incident which occurred about seventeen years ago. I don't believe I will hurt any one's feelings now by mentioning it. The professor of elocution was sick one day, and the boys came after me. They wanted me to come because the teacher was away, and I resolved to go and entertain that class and let it pass for a recitation. Professors often do that. When I came into the class-room, I said to the boy on the front seat: "What was the last lesson you had in elocution?" One of the boys said:

"Peter Piper, pickle-picker, picked six pecks of pickled peppers;
If Peter Piper, pickle-picker, picked six pecks of pickled peppers,
Where are the six pecks of pickled peppers which Peter Piper picked?"

OBSERVATION:—

That is "lip exercise" in elocution. I said to that young man, "I will not teach elocution. But I wish you would come up and deliver that to this class just as you would to an audience." The boy came up and put his toes together, and his hands by his side, for he had not reached the study of gesture. He yelled very rapidly and loudly:

"Peter Piper, pickle-picker, picked six pecks of pickled peppers;
If Peter Piper, piping, picked six pecks of pickled peppers,
Where are the pecks of pickled peppers which Peter Piper picked?"

It was elocution, but it was not oratory. I had trouble in getting up another boy, but I finally did. He thought that oratory consisted entirely in elocutionary "inflections," so he delivered it:

"Peter Piper picked six pecks of pickled peppers;
If Peter piping picked a peck of pickled peppers,
Where's the peck of pickled peppers Peter Piper picked?"

(With marked raising and lowering of the voice.)

It sounded like an old rooster in the barn in the morning. But being elocution, it was not oratory.

EVERY MAN HIS OWN UNIVERSITY

But the most illustrative and most absurd speech
I ever heard was by a visitor in that class that day.
He was sitting over near the aisle, and one of
the students came and whispered to me: "That
young man has graduated from an Eastern school
of elocution, and he is going to act the heavy parts
in tragedy upon the stage. He is a great elocutionist, and won't you get him to recite something to
the class?" I fell into the trap, and went down to
the young man, and said: "I understand you are
an elocutionist. Will you come up and recite
something for the class?"

As soon as he looked up at me I saw by his eyes
there was something the matter with his head. I
do not know just what, but things have happened
since that make it no unkindness to refer to him
the way I do. I said: "Please come up and recite something," and he replied: "Shall I recite
the same thing the young men have been reciting?" I said, "You don't need to do that;
take anything." He left his gold-headed cane—
the best part of him—on the floor, and then he
came up to the platform and leaned on the table
and said to me: "Shall I recite the same thing
the young men have been reciting?" I said:
"You can if you wish. You are perfectly free to
take anything you choose. The professor is away,

49

anyhow. When the cat is away the mice will play."

Then he began to prepare himself for that recitation. I never saw such behavior in my life. He pulled up his sleeves, brushed back his hair, shook himself, moved the table away forward, and I slid far back by the door and left the platform open, for I didn't know what he was going to do next. Then he gave the selection:

"Peter Piper picked a peck of pickled pepper-r-rs;
If Peter Piper, piping piper, picked a peck of pickled pepper-r-r-rs,
Where's the peck of pickled pepper-r-r-rs Peter Piper pickle-picker-r-r picked?"

He rolled in a flutter the letter "r" in each line. That class looked up with awe, and applauded until he repeated it. It was still elocution, but it was not oratory. He thought that oratory consisted of rolling the "r's" and rolling himself. That is not oratory.

Where do they learn oratory? They learn it in the old-fashioned school-house, from that old hen at the kitchen door, in some back office, in some hall, or some church where young men or women get together and debate, saying naturally the things they mean, and then *take notice* of the effects of what they debate upon, the conviction or after action of those who listen. That is the place to observe. You must *take notice* if you are to be a great orator.

The greatest orator of the future will be a woman. It has not been two months since the management of a women's Chautauqua said, "We could give $40,000 a year to any woman who will be a natural woman on the platform." They would make money at $40,000 a year if they hired a woman who would be a real woman. The trouble is that when women get on the platform they try to sing bass or try to speak as a man speaks. And there is such a need for women orators now! I get provoked about it when I think. Why isn't there a great woman orator like Mrs. Livermore now when she is needed so much?

OBSERVATION:—

VI

WOMAN'S INFLUENCE

IF women vote they will be of little account unless they are leaders. It is of no special advantage to the voter to ignorantly put a piece
of paper in a box. But it is of great account to
influence ten thousand votes. That is what
women must do if they are going to exercise their
right under suffrage—they must be the influence
behind the throne, not merely a voter.

When I was a boy in the district school a substitute teacher came in, and we all loved that little
woman. We would do anything she asked us to
do. One day that substitute teacher, who could
not get a first-class certificate, copied a verse of
a poem and asked me to read it:

> If you cannot on the ocean
>   Sail among the swiftest fleet:
> Rocking on the mighty billows,
>   Laughing at the storms you meet.

EVERY MAN HIS OWN UNIVERSITY

She asked me to read it once, and then she turned the paper over and said, "Now, Russell, repeat it." I said, "I have not learned it by heart." Said she: "Don't learn it by heart. I will try again." So she wrote the second verse:

> If you are too weak to journey
> Up the mountain steep and high.

Then she said to me, "Now, Russell, read it through once, and notice carefully each word, and don't look back at a word a second time." I know not now why she demanded that; I have looked in many books of psychology and in many places to find out. I have no explanation of this, and I ask you to think for me, for this is the fact. I took the second verse and read it through as she told me to do. Then she turned it over and said, "Please repeat it." I said, "I cannot repeat it; I have not learned it by heart." She replied: "Don't you say that again. Just shut your eyes and make a mental effort to see those verses, and then read it."

I shut my eyes and said, "Oh, it is all dark." Then she seemed very much disturbed and said: "Now, Russell, don't say that. Won't you try to do what I ask you to do?"

I thought the little woman was going to cry,

so I said, "Yes, I will do the best I can." She said, "Shut your eyes again and make a determined effort, with your eyes shut, to see that poetry just as though it were right before you." I shut my eyes and made that effort, and saw it as distinctly as though I had held it before my open eyes. So long as my eyes were shut I could see the two verses, and I read it all through, word for word, and I read it backward, word for word, to the beginning.

I thought I had seen a ghost. I went home and told my father what had happened, and he rushed down from the pasture to the schoolhouse and said to the teacher:

"If you indulge again in your foolish superstitions you will never teach in that schoolhouse again."

It must have been uncomfortable for her, and her secret went down to the grave with her, as far as I know. Yet what would I not give if I could place before the world now what that little girl knew. All our educational institutions, for which I have labored all these years, would be as nothing compared with that one secret if I could give it to you—that secret of being able to look upon a scene and shut's one's eyes and bring it all back again, study it in detail.

EVERY MAN HIS OWN UNIVERSITY

I have not had great personal power in that line. But I have seen a man who would take a column of the morning paper and read it down, and hand me the paper and read it through with his eyes shut and scarcely make a mistake. I do not know that I ever saw any one who was infallible, but rarely would he make a mistake. Often he could tell me where the comma, semicolon, and other marks of punctuation were.

I do not believe there is a normal child who is not mentally capable of that power when he has a teacher who understands how to develop it. That little teacher, who held only a second-class certificate, knew more about pyschology than many of the greatest men who preside over great institutions.

In the Alps some years ago was Professor Slayton, a native of Brighton, England. He was one of the nation's best botanists. His wife died and he was left with a little child between five and six years of age. They boarded at the Hotel Des Alps, in the Chamouni Valley. One morning he took his little girl up to the Mer-de-Glace, and then he told her to run back to the hotel, saying he would return to her in the evening.

She bid her father good-by and saw him go up Mont Blanc into the forest, and she ran back.

OBSERVATION:—

He did not return in the evening, and she sat up all night and worried, and early in the morning she ran out from the hotel and ran up the stream to the path she had seen her father take. Then, running across, she started climbing up the side of the great snow-capped mountain. She came suddenly to a place where the path ran around along a projecting precipice, two hundred and eighty feet in the perpendicular, around a promontory of rock that set a few feet back. When she came to that spot her feet slipped upon the snow on the glare ice, and she slid down and down over the edge so far that her fingers just caught in the moss on the edge and one foot rested on about an inch projection of the rock.

As she hung there she screamed, "Papa!" Her father heard that cry. He was down in the valley so far that he could not see her, but he could hear her voice. He recognized it, and he felt there was an awful need of him—"humanity called to him." He ran across the valley and up the path. On the way there was a tree near which he had previously *noticed* there was an ax. He pulled out the ax and ran on to a tree where he had previously *observed* there was a rope which the coal-burners had long used to let coal down from the cliff. He clipped the rope with the ax, threw away the ax, and, tying the rope around him as he had *noticed* the guides do who take travelers over the "sea of ice," he ran on, until suddenly he came to the spot where his little girl had slipped. He could see the parting in her hair twenty feet down, and all was glare ice between. His heart must have stopped beating. But he suddenly shouted:

"Papa's come. Hold on tight!"

She screamed, "I cannot hold on any longer!"

He turned and threatened her. Oh, ye parents, whosoever you may be, you may save your own son or daughter from a physical or moral death by training them to obey when they are young. Her fingers tightened again, and he threw the rope around the butt of a tree he had *noticed*, and let himself rapidly down over that ice. He tried to get hold of his little child's hands, but they had melted deep into the moss, and he let himself down beside her and caught hold of her dress and pulled her to him.

Both were hanging from the edge of the cliff, and the end of the rope was in his hand, and his hand on the ice. He tried to pull himself up, but the rope would not give an inch, and then he tried to push his little girl up, but with frozen fingers she could not climb.

OBSERVATION:—

There they hung in the high Alps, alone! Will he fall on the jagged rocks and be crushed to death? No, he will not fall, because he is a king. He has used his *every-day observation*, though he is a graduate of a university. He had *noticed* something more—he had observed how the dogs howl when they find perishing travelers. Those St. Bernard dogs, whenever they find a dead body or a man laying insensible, will always howl in one peculiar way. Those dogs know more about acoustics than an architect. How do they know? God told them. When a dog utters that cry it can be heard for miles and miles. The professor imitated the call of the dog, and when it rang down the valley the coal-burners heard it and the wood-choppers heard it. They said:

"That is a dog, and a dog never howls like that unless he has found a dying man." So, throwing down their axes and guns, and running over the snows toward the sound of the call, they suddenly came to the spot. They caught hold of the rope and one of them slid down rapidly and seized the little girl's arm and passed her up, and then caught hold of the professor's arm and lifted him, while the others pulled upon the rope. Thus they dragged him up. The professor fell on the snow-drift and fainted dead away.

EVERY MAN HIS OWN UNIVERSITY

But he was a king. He heard humanity's cry, and when he heard it he knew where the ax was. He had used his every-day study in such a way that he knew where the old rope was, and knew how to tie it, and he knew how to call for help. Whenever you find on earth a successful man or woman you will always find it is a man or woman who hears humanity's call, and who has so used his every-day means of observation that he knows where the weapons are with which to fight those battles, or where the means are with which to bring men relief.

I could not better put into your minds that professor's feelings than by a quotation of an English phrase which he printed in English on his scientific books, though the books were published in French:

We live for those who love us,
    For those who know us true;
For the heavens that bend above us,
    For the good that we can do.
For the wrongs that lack resistance,
For each cause that needs assistance,
For the future in the distance,
    For the good that we can do.

VII

EVERY MAN'S UNIVERSITY

A DISTINCT university walks about under each man's hat. The only man who achieves success in the other universities of the world, and in the larger university of life, is the man who has first taken his graduate course and his post-graduate course in the university under his hat. There *observation* furnishes a daily change in the curriculum. Books are not the original sources of power, but observation, which may bring to us all wide experience, deep thinking, fine feeling, and the power to act for oneself, is the very dynamo of power.

Without observation, literature and meditation are shower and sunshine upon unbroken soil. Only those schools and colleges are true schools and colleges which regard it as the chief business of all their teaching to persuade those under their charge to see more perfectly what they are looking at, to find what they should have been unable to observe had it not been for their school instruction. You can't make a good arrow from a pig's tail, and you can seldom get a man worth while out of one who has gone through the early part of his life without having learned to be alert when things are to be seen or heard. John Stuart Blackie says that it is astonishing how much we all go about with our eyes wide open and see nothing, and Doctor Johnson says that some men shall see more while riding ten miles upon the top of an omnibus, than some others shall see in riding over the continent.

How to observe should be the motto, not only in the beginning of our life, but throughout our career. With the same intellectual gifts, interested in the same ideas, two men walk side by side through the same scenery and meet the same people. One man has had much inspiration from the country traversed, and has been intent upon all that he has seen and heard among the people. The other has caught no inspiration from beauty or bird or blossom, and only the trivialities of the people have amused him.

A traveler in Athens or Rome, Paris or London, may be shown these cities by a professional guide, and yet gain only a smattering of what these cities hold in store for him, and remember little of what he has seen. Another traveler, un-attended by a guide, but observant of everything that comes to his eyes and ears, will carry away stores from his visit to those cities, which shall be of life-long interest and be serviceable to all who shall travel his way. The solitary but observant stranger in a country almost always profits most from his travels. He is compelled to notice boulevards and buildings, parks and people; and every day of his travels is a lesson in observation that accustoms him to remember all he has once seen. The newspaper correspondents of other days had no guide-books or guides, and they were entire strangers in the places they visited. They relied entirely upon themselves to find their way, and to discover everything that was valuable and interesting. They found much that the modern guide either overlooks or disregards, and wrote for the papers at home what would most interest and instruct their readers.

When Henry M. Stanley first visited Jerusalem he insisted that the dragoman in charge of his party should keep all guides and guide-books out of his sight. In two days Stanley knew the streets and the location of the Temple and the Holy Sepulcher and all the notable places in that old city. If Stanley is to-day known as one of the most intelligent of travelers, it is mainly because he excelled in daily *observation*, which every one who thinks for himself recognizes as the supreme acquisition of a liberal education. He often said that he knew Rome, Naples, and Vienna far better than he knew New York, where he had lived many years of his life. In that he resembled the rest of humanity, who generally know less about what is notable in their home places, than observant visitors know who stay there only a short time during their travels. What we pay for in time and labor seems more valuable—nothing pay, nothing value.

A great foreign correspondent of his day, Henry W. Chambers, remained only six hours at Baalbek, near Damascus; yet he wrote the clearest description that probably ever was written of the magnificent temples at Baalbek—and he wrote these descriptions, too, at Hong-Kong, after many and varied experiences while visiting other places of greater importance. Many archeologists and literary men before him had visited the moat of the great fortress at Baalbek. Still, they had never observed as Chambers observed, and so they missed seeing the arrow-heads and all the other warlike instruments used in those ancient days, which had lain unnoticed among those huge pillars and great foundation-stones.

5

OBSERVATION:—

Although General Lew Wallace lived a long time at Jerusalem, he only imagined that there might have been an inner dungeon underneath the great prison; so when he wrote *Ben Hur* he put his leprous heroine into this imaginary prison-house. A school-teacher from northern England, with her tourist-candle, afterward found the doorway of this prison which Wallace had only imagined to be there. On their way from Egypt and Palestine to the Euphrates, travelers had for centuries passed over the same path in the desert; but it was reserved for a cutter of marble inscriptions, after all these centuries, to *observe* the Rosetta Stone, by the help of which archeologists can now read the inscriptions upon the tablets in the ancient palaces of Babylon and Nineveh.

Millions and millions had seen the lid of a teakettle bobbing up and down over the boiling water before that Scotchman, Watt, observed it while making watches. But he was the first of all those millions whose close observation led him to investigate this force of boiling water in the teakettle. Then he applied this power to the steam-engine, which is still the great propelling force of the world. From the time of the Garden of Eden apples had fallen in the orchards of the world, through all the harvest-days. Of all the billions that had seen apples falling, only Sir Isaac Newton observed the law of gravitation that was involved in their falling.

All the great discoverers began with nearly the same meager powers for observation that the rest of the world has, but early in life came to value above all other mental powers this incalculable power to closely notice; and each made his realm of observation much richer for his discoveries.

Why do the majority of us go through life seeing nothing of the millions of marvelous truths and facts while only a few keep their eyes and ears wide open and every day are busy in piling up what they have observed! The loss of our instincts seems to be the price we pay to-day for the few minor acquisitions we get from school and college; we put out our brains to make room for our learning. The man who assiduously cultivates his powers of observation and thus gains daily from his experiences what helps him to see farther and clearer everything in life that is worth seeing, has given himself a discipline that is much more important than the discipline of all the schools and the colleges without it. The greatest text-books of the greatest universities are only the records of the observations of some close observer whose

OBSERVATION:—

better powers of seeing things had been acquired mainly while he was taking his courses in that university under his hat.

The intellect is both telescope and microscope; if it is rightly used, it shall observe thousands of things which are too minute and too distant for those who with eyes and ears neither see nor hear. The intellect can be made to look far beyond the range of what men and women ordinarily see; but not all the colleges in the world can alone confer this power—this is the reward of *self-culture;* each must acquire it for himself; and perhaps this is why the power of observing deeply and widely is so much oftener found in those men and those women who have never crossed the threshold of any college but the University of Hard Knocks.

> The quickening power of science only he
> Can know, from whose *own* soul it gushes free.

When we look back over our life and reflect how many things we might have seen and heard had we trained our powers of observation, we seem to have climbed little and to have spent most of our time upon plateaus, while our achievements seem little better than scratches upon black marble. Mankind has a greater esteem for the degrees conferred by the University of Observation and Experience than for all the other degrees of all other Universities in the world. The only thing that seems most to win the respect of real men and women for the degrees conferred by colleges is the fact that the graduates have first gained all that close observation and wide experience can confer.

The lives of the men and the women who have been worth while keep reminding us how vastly more important is this education from ceaseless observation than all the mere learning from school courses. It takes ten pounds of the stuff gotten from observation and experience to carry one pound of school learning wisely. The thinking man will never ask you what college you have gone through, but what college has gone through you; and the ability and habit of observing deeply and broadly is the preparation we all need that the college may go through us. Confucius of China, Kito of Japan, Goethe of Germany, Arnold of England, Lincoln and Edison of America, stand where they stand today in thought and action solely because they had in a masterly way educated their power of minute attention. In building up a huge business or in amassing enormous riches, such men as Roth-

OBSERVATION:—

schild, Rockefeller, and Carnegie show us especially how vitally important to all material success is steadfast attendance at the school of attention.

The colleges that to-day are advancing most rapidly in esteem are those which are recognizing more and more the importance of observation. They require their men to spend some portion of their college time in gaining experience in their various lines through observing the practical workings of their calling; medical students are in hospitals; students of law attend courts; theological students engage in mission work; and engineers are found in shops. Neither lectures nor speculations can take the place of these experiences; each is helpful to the other. When only one may be had, the experience from observing actual work is far more important. Opportunities for observation of practical matters, along with theory, is the modern idea toward which all the best modern institutions are tending in their efforts to fit men for the active business of life.

Nor has greatness from careful observation and large experience distinguished men of action alone. Shakespeare, Goethe, Bunyan, Burns, Whittier, Longfellow, James Whitcomb Riley,

EVERY MAN HIS OWN UNIVERSITY

and a host of the great men of philosophy, science, and literature are where they are to-day in the esteem of their fellow men, and in their service to humanity, because they were the keenest among the men acute in observation.

VIII

ANIMALS AND "THE LEAST THINGS"

THE benefits brought to humanity through the study of lower animal life are incalculable, and could not be told in one book. With all that vivisection and post-morten dissection have revealed to scientific examiners, contagious and infectious diseases have been nearly removed from the human family. We have been taught to live better from observing animal habits in searching for food, in building their habitats, in their mode of living, in their fear of man, and in the methods they adopt to preserve their health. All this knowledge has been gained for us, for the upbuilding of humanity, through the efforts of *close observers*. They have studied the cat by the hearth, the dog by the door, the horses in the pasture and stall, the pigs in their pens, and the sheep in their folds. Closely associated with the investigators of animal life are those who have observed the origin, habits, and influence of birds, insects, and creeping things.

But what we have learned from animals in the past seems only a trifle in comparison with what they will teach when we go to them with more serious purpose and more carefully observe them. The leaders in all these investigations of animal life have all been distinguished for their power to discover in animals what has escaped other people.

Professor Darwin's close observation of the doves he fed at his door opened up to him important suggestions and laid the foundation for his great treatise, "The Origin of Species." When Professor Niles of the Boston School of Technology was a boy he caught a minnow while returning from school. At his father's suggestion he put the fish into a simple aquarium and studied its movements. When it died he carefully examined its parts under a microscope—and this experience was the beginning of his vast knowledge of the animal realm.

While a Philadelphia clergyman was visiting a farmer in northern New Jersey, the family became perturbed because their dog had "gone mad." They fastened it in the kitchen and sought somebody to kill it by shooting at it through the window. A neighbor observed the dog carefully and told them it was poisoned. He advised the family to loose it in order that it might get some antidote

OBSERVATION:—

for itself in field or forest. He told them that
cats, cattle, and horses are often compelled to find
an antidote for some poisonous herb they have
eaten, and that the animals know more about
such things than any teacher in the medical
schools. As soon as the dog was unfastened he
hastened across the field to a brook, and ate a weed
that was growing beside the water. The dog
soon returned to the house, and ate heartily after
a two weeks' fast.

The clergyman had followed the dog and observed the plant which it had eaten. After the
dog had returned to the house he uprooted the
plant and took some of its leaves to a Philadelphia
firm of chemists. Acting upon the firm's advice,
he sent the leaves to the Smithsonian Institution
at Washington, and they were found to be a valuable antidote for poison. Not only was humanity
given a better medicine from this discovery, but
the clergyman also derived a competency from
it. This remedy for poisoning is often used in
prescriptions; so even doctors sometimes "go to
the dogs" for instructions.

Like Professor Agassiz and Sir Oliver Lodge,
many find their best instructors in domestic
animals. The fowls around the house and the
barn may be whole universities for developing

the sciences. Through her dependence on nature the hen is a more efficient instructor than the majority of college professors. She knows by instinct so much of the laws of nature that wise men may sit at her feet or her bill and learn. Perhaps she may seem a little foolish in proclaiming her achievements in egg-laying by a cackle, but her knowledge of the necessities of life, her careful oversight of her brood, the way she uses her feet and her wings, her foreknowledge of approaching storms, her means of defending herself when attacked by hawks, her knowledge of the formation of the egg and of the proper time to break the shell for the release of her chick—all these are worthy of the attention of even the greatest scientists.

In an address at a poultry-men's convention, Oliver Wendell Holmes said that chickens seem to have in them much more to study than did Darwin's doves. While Holmes was once summering at Kennebunkport, Maine, he trained five chickens to come at his call, to fly upon his head, and to leap with open bills to catch a kernel of corn. Before the season closed the chickens would come to his bedroom even after he had retired—making it necessary, as Doctor Holmes said, for the landlord to serve them up for dinner. Doctor Holmes's

OBSERVATION:—

parody on Longfellow's "A Psalm of Life" shows what a careful observer he was. While some of Longfellow's admirers resented the parody as a slight, Longfellow himself always treated it as complimentary. He once told James T. Fields that, in one couplet of the parody, Holmes had excelled the entire original poem:

> Not like muffled drums be beating
> On the inside of the shell.

Longfellow told Fields that there are always millions of men standing like chickens in the shell, with wings they know not how to use, having calls to a larger life outside of which they can see nothing; that some peck away until dead on the inside of the shell, while others, assisted by a friend on the outside, step out into a life beautiful and complete.

In the egg or molecule we get nearer to God than we do through the telescope or by encircling the earth. He who lived nearest the first cause gets the best inspiration for visions of all greater sights or events; so the cottage is a happier place than the palace for him who wishes to get better acquainted with what shall arouse finer thought and feeling. The cottage is the best preparatory school for the mansion, provided always that the cottage course has been thorough. He who has worn his cottage life with manly dignity shall be the man to wear his mansion life with composure. Emerson said "the entire system of things gets represented in every particle."

Uneasy is the head that wears the crown, and unfortunate is the man who gets a smattering of many things yet does not know even one small thing thoroughly. The power of little things to give instruction and happiness should be the first lesson in life, and it should be inculcated deeply. The chief need of this discontented and sinful world is to comprehend that in one blade of grass or the shading of an evening cloud there is sufficient reverence to fill the largest heart, and sufficient science to occupy the greatest passion.

We saw a delicate blue flower in the grass this morning which I had never noticed before. It seemed a different flower from each angle and, when put under a magnifying-glass, had colors I had never noticed before in flower or art. The field where it was growing had been familiar to me for threescore years and ten, yet the flower was entirely new to me. It was so dainty and attractive and inspiring that I felt I had lost something important to my spiritual growth all these years—something like the experience of Virgil,

Guizot, Carlyle, Grotius, or like Tennyson in the "Holy Grail," who declares that he had left a real and wonderful life behind to follow the unknown. This little flower in the morning sunlight awakes thoughts of years long past—of the faces of marshaled hosts of battle, of eyes deep and calm with the smile of a loving mother's welcome, of the great forgiveness in a father's affection.

Had I found that flower seventy years before, I believe my appreciation of the Divine Power would have been greater, my heart would have been more satisfied, my soul more fully illuminated and pervaded by a holier peace. We lose ourselves in all attempts to grasp the cause of which this small flower is the result. It is impossible to find words to convey the strange emotions which this newly found flower aroused, and to tell of the distant realms my imagination visited while I meditated there. If we would free ourselves from the perplexing cares which our daily duties demand; if we would forget the worries of each day; if the losses and disappointments and the wrongs of many years did not press themselves upon us; if the demands of many duties and the demands upon our attention and the calls of friends did not interrupt—we could find in contemplating this wee flower of the field a fund of happiness which years of sorrow and misfortune could not destroy.

Bacon and Burke and Niebuhr discovered how much of grandeur can come into a life from the little things about us, but they all discovered it when it was too late to go back and live the *ideal* life of simplicity and individuality which was suggested to them by a drop of water and a humming-bird. The smallest things are the largest in importance, if they bring into our lives the largest thoughts and feelings and an incentive to largest actions for self and humanity. Why are we forever looking upon the horizon for what upon closer view lies at our feet? These little beauties of the field rebuke the wanderer and the eminent man when it says to all the world, with a sweet smile and a dainty pout, "You could have found more in my life than has ever been learned from the sages."

While Zinzendorf was stranded nearly a year upon a tiny island, his vigorous mind was forced to occupy itself in observing the objects upon the shore; his examinations of the colors in the clamshell led him to say later in life, at a meeting of philosophers, that a lifetime study of these colors should develop more of the beautiful than all the manufactured color combinations then known.

OBSERVATION:—

Art has not yet been able to combine the shades shown in the shell of an oyster, and the wings of the June bug have been enlarged and copied by colored photography, and will greatly influence all art hereafter. Man's needs shall be best supplied by beginning at the source and following the Creator in developing them into things of beauty and service.

Although the Agricultural Department at Washington spent eight million dollars in the study of seeds and their growth by sending experts to roam over the world for investigations, yet the observations of Luther Burbank and many like investigators in the agricultural colleges throughout the country have made many more important discoveries. Their observations have brought about a greater increase of production to the acre than all the results of those who roamed the earth for the Government, and no one would say that their work was not a fair investment for the nation.

Observation convinces us that the sooner we get down to the simplicities of life, the longer and healthier and nobler shall life become. The healthiest are those with one loaf and a natural hunger along with it. The noblest lives are those who are anxious to become as divine as it is possible for them to be, are ever alert for little deeds of kindness. How much richer life the poet lives who can sympathize with the field-mouse, like Burns! Who is lifted heavenward by the fringed gentian, like Bryant? Who gets the messages of peace from the frosted pumpkin, like Riley? Like Shakespeare, we too may "find tongues in trees, books in running brooks, sermons in stones, and good in everything," if we will but use our eyes for seeing, our ears for hearing, our heads for understanding, and our hearts for feeling. The Poor Man's University gives its courses everywhere, and no entrance examination is requisite other than a mind willing to concentrate upon the sublime objects which, by the million, lie within our vision.

6

IX

THE BOTTOM RUNG

ALMOST every day of his life an American is reminded that "necessity is the mother of invention." It needs only a little reflection and observation to realize how much American youth are blessed in the examples of their countrymen who have come from the humblest stations in life and have risen through sheer pluck and perseverance to honor and helpfulness.

We are indebted mainly to the genius and the observation of poor men for the great inventions which have so much contributed to the comfort, the convenience, the cheerfulness, and the power of life. They have given us steam as a motive power, the locomotive, the telegraph, the typewriter, the telephone, the automobile, the victrola, the airship. The great advances that have been made in agriculture through mowers, reapers, planters, and special seeds and fruits are entirely the results of their steadfast perseverance. Nobody ever earnestly reaches out for a thing until he feels that he needs it, consequently, the sons and daughters of the rich are seldom the benefactors of humanity in the way so many poor men and women have been through the inventions which have lightened the drudgery of millions of homes, as well as increased marvelously the productions of the soil and of the factory. Had the talents of the rich been put to the test by hunger or cold or the many other incentives to vigorous thought and action which impel the poor, they also might have many inventions to their credit, for the longing of the normal soul furnishes the basis of all the worthy activities of life.

The greatest drawback for rich men's sons and daughters is in having all their wants supplied from the bank-account of indulgent parents. They are taught neither industry, economy, nor self-control, which often makes them a social menace. They lack appreciation for so many of the things in life which help to brighten the path of the poor, solely because they have never needed them. A hungry boy who has stood on the outside of a bakery, clinging to a nickel and fighting a battle with himself whether to invest it in a bit of bread or to take it home to his mother, who has had neither breakfast nor dinner, fully understands the value of a dollar.

OBSERVATION:—

The superintendent of the Patent Office at Washington has confirmed the official report of the French Patent Office—that there has been no invention of especial value which has not been either found or improved upon by some poor man. The best life-preserver was invented by a sailor who had fallen overboard and had been nearly drowned. An obscure native of a duchy bordered on three sides by powerful nations invented the quick-firing gun, which can fire six hundred shots while the ordinary gun is being loaded. It was a poor Cambridge machinist, whose family often suffered from lack of food, who invented the sewing-machine, which has changed the condition of home life throughout the world, and relieved women of one of their great household burdens. The ship's chronometer was made practical for navigation by a man who had been lost at sea and despaired of ever again reaching the shore. The locomotive, which has contributed more than any other one thing to the spread of our people over our vast country, was given to the world by an Englishman, Stephenson, who in early life had been so poor that he had little schooling.

More than eight hundred agricultural inventions were patented in 1905 and 1906, and every one of them is the invention of some poor man or woman.

As inventors, women have in recent years become close competitors of men, and from kitchen utensils to floor covering have added much to home comfort and home furnishing. All the household articles exhibited lately in a large shop in Chicago were either invented or improved by women. They have invented many things for agriculture, for manufacturing, and for school furnishings—and not a few of the great patents which have been issued to men should have been issued to their wives. Women have often awaked an idea which men have wrought out for practical purposes. The majority of the benefactors of the world made their discoveries to relieve some necessity which oppressed them personally. This is especially true of stockbreeding, where the improvements of observant men have so greatly increased the value of domestic animals.

The value of any study depends entirely upon what it has done for us and what we are doing with it. Lowell says that mere learning is as insignificant as the collection of old postage-stamps. Professor Virchow was obliged to try various foods in his experiments with his own cats, before he discovered what has ever since been of such benefit to all breeders of animals throughout the world. From the earliest days the bee has offered a store of the most useful information, but it would never have been known had it not been for such patient observers as Huber, who, although blind, discovered more about bees than the world had ever known before his day, through the patient service of his wife and valet. The mouse ' in the field, the squirrel in the tree, the eagle in her nest, the fish in the brook, all have taught us valuable lessons in conduct. They have doubt- less given hints which have enabled observant men to give mankind many a useful invention.

When we consider the many thousands of useful inventions which have added so much to the con- venience and the happiness of life, and when we bring to mind how almost all of these have come from the humblest of the sons of men with none of the advantages of the so-called higher educa- tion, of which we hear so much to-day, we are forced to agree with Sir Walter Scott that the best part of every man's education is that which he gives himself independent of text-books other than the Book of Life. Every real man and woman attends a school or college, not to learn, but to learn how to learn. This is the best work that schools of any description can do. It lays a firm foundation upon which the man who has learned how to learn can build his own superstructure. The men who have achieved success in the march of the ages are those who have been the architects of their own life. Nobody cares a fig where we get our educational tools. The world is interested only in what we are doing with them. *We* must be *self-made* or *never-made*, whether we go to college or work in the fields. One teacher can be serviceable to a thousand of the sort who intend to make themselves, but a thousand teachers cannot help one of the other sort. Heredity and environment and will are the great deciding factors in every life.

Investigations as to the food values of meats, grains, fruits, vegetables, and other foods are now being made by the Government, by colleges, and other investigators. This is the movement of *supreme* importance for the uplift of humanity. But the most of this kind of investigating has been done in household kitchens. It is probable that many of the greatest discoveries as to food will hereafter be made in the same places by those who are inclined to observe. The need of closer scientific knowledge of the chemistry of digestion and the chemistry of food is vital; it should call forth the most self-sacrificing investigation.

It is said by those who have carefully studied the subject that ninety-one per cent. of all disease is attributable directly or indirectly to the stomach. Our ailments come mainly from our aliments. Nourishing food is an essential of a noble life. The stomach is the master of the house, and must be respected. A proper diet and a sound head are closely allied, and those who will rightly exercise their soul-powers must be watchful of the stomach.

Those who would rule and lead must have chest and stomach as well as head and will.

Nobody else has such opportunities for observing the effects of food, and for studying the happy results of nutritious food, as those have who prepare the meals in the kitchen. Proper nourishment is something which touches humanity on every side, and deserves the closest attention of the greatest minds. We can better afford to dispense with scientific experts in every other line which now engages them than to dispense with those who investigate the food question. The idea among the myriads of American housekeepers, that it is ignoble drudgery to spend some of their time in their kitchens ministering to the health of those who are nearest and dearest to them and removing diseases from them through well-selected and well-cooked food, is being gradually overcome by many schools and colleges. The sciences connected with food are now placed among the most important subjects in the curricula of these schools. It takes a master mind to handle the chemical combinations of the kitchen, which make hale and happy men and women, boys and girls.

Health is symmetry; disease is deformity; both are mainly the result of what we eat.

Food has killed more than the sword in every age, and is perhaps killing more to-day than ever before. Achievement in soul-growth and material-growth is involved in the question of proper food. If women forsake the throne that rightly belongs to the cook, men must assume it or Christian civilization shall cease. To-day nobody can become so supreme a benefactor of humanity as the man or the woman who devotes intellect and all other power to the study of scientific eating. When we come rightly to understand all the vital questions that are involved in nutrition, we shall feel that the kings among men and the queens among women are to be sought in no higher place than in kitchens.

OBSERVATION:—

We are forever searching among the stars to discover kings, when they are far oftener found in cottages in the valley.

If universities fail to make the knowledge of the right nutrition practical and fail to bring it down where humble men and women may get it and apply it, the fault is their own. Some day a people grateful for the health they enjoy may elect a man to the Presidency of our nation, or set him upon some throne, because he is the best scientific cook in the land. Doctor Agnew of Philadelphia said that he had gained his most important knowledge of hospital work as an adviser of the dietitians while feeding his dog and his cat.

In speaking of the discovery of radium by Madame Curie, Professor Virchow said that he had often felt that our investigators had not taken sufficient notice of the force of animal electricity. The few experiments already made in applying to machinery electricity generated by the human body has opened up a field for observant scientists.

In many ways both birds and beasts contribute to the welfare of humanity, and the observing thinker will still find many more ways in which he can aid us. All forms of life can be harnessed to the car of civilization, and far more effective work shall be done than is being done to-day. As teachers and as subjects of practical investigation, animals supply a great university which almost every man and woman can attend.

X

HOME READING

CARLYLE says that a collection of books is a true university in these days. It might be added that often the smaller the collection the larger shall be the university.

Education derived from libraries is unsafe, for book-dissipation, as well as drunkenness, ends in debauchery. Toward the end of his long and wide-awake life Doctor Holmes advised a young correspondent to confine his reading to the Bible, Shakespeare, and a good dictionary. The list of men who have been lifted to higher regions of thought and feeling and action from reading any one of these three would be too long to be compressed within the covers of one book. Books are like two-edged swords—dangerous unless one knows how to use them; they either lead up or drag down, and we sink or rise to the level of the books we read. Every one reads, but how many read to advantage? Goethe, the greatest of all the very greatest Germans, said, "I have been learning how to read for the past fifty years, but have not yet succeeded."

The majority of readers resemble hour-glasses—their reading runs in and out, and leaves no traces; and some others are like housewives' jelly-bags—they pass all that is good, and retain only the refuse. At best, only a small percentage of our life is spent in school; the greater part of the remainder each must pass in the University of Daily Life, where our education is derived from experience gained through *close observation* in daily contact with our fellows, and from the fellowship of books. Fellowship fits the relation perfectly, for there must be intimate intercourse such as this word implies, or *nothing*. It is with books as with life—a man profits little from being merely *acquainted* with ten thousand, and he may be incalculably injured from his intercourse with them; but a few *choice* friends—often the *fewer* the better—bring a steady growth of higher spiritual power greater than can be had from all other influences combined.

So it is with books. Acquaintance with a thousand often renders a capable man impotent. But a few *choice* friends with whom he frequently and earnestly communes lift him in strength of intellect and will and tenderness and sweetness of feeling to be the peer of the worthiest.

The beginning of New England was the golden age of scholarship in America, for many of the founders of these colonies had been reared in English universities. Such was the struggle in these bleak and barren colonies for existence during the first years, that in a few generations the majority of their posterity were strangers to almost all the books of *power* and *knowledge* with which their forefathers were acquainted, and were forced to glean all they harvested from the Bible and the almanac—especially the almanac. The almanac was eagerly perused by every member of the family from the dawn of the year to its setting. The reputed thrift of the plain people in this corner of the great world is largely attributable to the lessons of the almanac—mainly *Poor Richard's Almanac*, which the Bostonian, Franklin, annually edited in Philadelphia for over a quarter of a century. His chief purpose was to drive home forcibly many lessons which might encourage the colonists to get the most out of their hard and isolated lives.

Peabody, the successful man of business and munificent philanthropist, said that an almanac and a jack-knife were the foundation of the education through which he ultimately did so much good for multitudes of his countrymen. It should be interesting and instructive to know how many more, during the "jack-knife epoch" in New England and the generations since that time, have been indebted to one book for the pluck and perseverance by which they have carved out a place of honor for themselves. Never were books so eagerly, so often, and so carefully read as these poor almanacs. Never, perhaps, has any other book except the Bible been so potent an influence in shaping the life of a nation and shaping it to a *high place among the nations*, whose beneficent influences have humanized the world. Many a writer has reminded us that the almanac was the text-book studied by our ancestry in beginning the enormous agricultural, commercial, mercantile, manufacturing, and financial interests which in four generations have placed us in front of the richest nations of the earth.

Think of the many millions of dollars invested in library-buildings and the many millions more invested in the books they shelter! Think of the five hundred millions spent annually in public education, and the hundreds of millions that have been put into college buildings and college breeding! Still, from all this stupendous investment there will never come men and women who will make any more out of their learning than thousands of men and women of colonial days who knew the contents of no books other than the Bible and the almanac.

The quality of the literary attainment of those reared in a library may be higher—and perhaps not; but wider and deeper self-knowledge, self-respect, self-confidence, self-culture, self-control, are the supreme objects of all life-struggle and educational struggle. Where a man gets the educational tools with which to accomplish all this is not at all important. If an almanac can help one man to get the same life-result as another man gets from the polishing of the greatest universities in the world, the almanac is the peer of the university. Whether materials as insignificant as the almanac have been used to attain just such results, the history of our country and of several other countries can readily prove. Three books made up the library of Lincoln, the rail-splitter, of Edison and Carnegie, the telegraph operators; but no three men of the nation were ever more successful in reaching the goals they set for themselves.

Books are to-day the great universal means of *knowing*, and knowing them depends upon reading them rightly. It is not so important how *many* books we read, but how we read them. A well-read fool is one of the most pestilential of blockheads. One book *read* avails more than a thousand *skimmed*. Little reading and much thinking make a wise man; much reading and little thinking has bred the race which the *plain* people call "learned fools," and these are mainly responsible for any ridicule that is put upon the work of school and college.

In these days when the printing-press has largely superseded the pulpit and the platform, it is vitally important that men shall be taught how to read rightly and shall be helped to habits of right reading; and no school or college that is decently interested in the welfare of the people can disregard this one duty of teachers *above all others*. Much of the best in thought and feeling and conduct shall depend hereafter upon the books which we read with careful observation. Every man who has read himself into higher realms is under bonds to make the source of so much bliss and blessedness as admirable and as desirable as possible to all who are strangers to the most pleasant and profitable paths of literature.

It is not the quantity of our reading, but the quality that makes it and us an influence for good

to our fellows. A man who has read ten pages
with real accuracy, says John Ruskin, is forever-
more in some measure an educated person. You
might read all the books in the British Museum,
yet be an utterly illiterate and uneducated person. Our reading without digestion and assimila-
tion is as useless as our food without them. Bacon
says that reading makes a *full* man; but fullness
without digestion is dyspepsia. The books whose
reading impels us to live nobly and do noble service for others, are *the* books, and it is a wicked
waste of time to read what is a negative quantity.
Whoever masters *one vital* book can never become
commonplace.

Thoroughness is the master-passion in reading,
as in every other undertaking. Those who have
accumulated wisdom, culture, power, riches, are
always prominent for their indefatigable, pains-
taking thoroughness; nothing to them is a trifle,
for "trifles make perfection, and perfection is no
trifle." Those who have thought most and felt
most and done most from their reading have
brought this master passion to it.

When we begin to become acquainted with all
the worthy men and women who trace the beginning of their worth to the careful reading of
one book, it seems almost a loss to the world to

have the libraries of the world so large. If they were all respectable occupants of their shelves, it might be condoned; but the copyright of millions of books is the only right, human or divine, for their existing at all. Many a country boy at the fireside during the long winter evenings has received inspiration from repeatedly reading one or two worthy books; these have spurred him on to fight his way valiantly through college, and from there to the heights in some worthy life-work.

If we are true to all that *manhood* involves, there is no self-deception in the conviction that each one of us is born for *kingship*. Supreme kingship "consists in a stronger *moral* state and a truer *thoughtful* state than that of other men, which enables us to *guide* and *raise* the misguided and the illiterate." Every thoughtful man and woman ultimately discovers that "all *education* and all *literature* are useful only so far as they confirm this calm and beneficent kingly power." Emerson's "man-thinking" is the supreme among human beings.

The best that can be known and experienced lies asleep in books, and one of the chief purposes for getting an education is to give us the *well-made* head and the *finer* feeling to awake this best knowledge and experience in these sleeping princes.

OBSERVATION:—

De Quincey reminds us that all the greatest books may be divided into the literature of *knowledge* and the literature of *power*. They have all been written in utmost sincerity by the *right*-minded and the *strong*-minded; they disclose boundless fields for soul-*refreshment* and soul-*expansion*. In the march of civilization, the men and the nations that have forged farthest ahead since Gutenberg invented printing are the men and the nations that have had most to do with the few books of *knowledge* and *power* of the greatest and the wisest. There can be no better test of a man's thought and feelings and actions than the books he reads and the books he keeps around him; and there is none so desolate as the poor *rich* man who lives in a great bookless house, and "has never fed upon the dainties that are bred in books," as John Milton says.

The very presence of books is refining, and the right kind of man would as soon think of building his house without windows as of furnishing it without books. In every well-regulated home of intelligent men and women the library is always one of the annual items of expenditure. When we have learned how to consult the books of *knowledge* and *power*, they let us mingle with the best society of all ages; they make the *mightiest* men and women of words and deeds our advisers; they bring us the gold of learning and the gems of thought; and they furnish us with the soul-*food* which brings the proper kind of soul-*growth*. Such books are the safest of companions, for they protect us from vice and the inferior passions; more than ever they are to-day *indispensable* for all who are striving to do the higher work of civilization and *Christianity*.

Every *real* book we *really* read gives us greater faith in the *goodness* and the *nobility* of life. As Lowell says, "Adds another block to the climbing spire of a great soul." The other sort which "swarm from the cozy marshes of immoral brains," the sort also who "rack their brains for lucre," do the devil's work for him, and are as baneful as the company of fools and vulgarians. Show an observant man your bookshelves, and he'll tell you what you are. The man who does not *love* some great book is not worth the time we spend in his company; we are fortunate if we are not in some way contaminated by him. If we knew the road they have traveled, we should likely find that those of modern times who have merited the crown of kings and queens for their stronger *moral* state and their *truer thoughtful* state have had most to do with some literature of knowledge and power; that they especially oftenest consulted the books of the greatest and wisest in their difficulties, and had been spurred on by their messages to the thoughts and the deeds which made them worthy.

It is fortunate that to-day the greatest of books are the common property of the printers of the world, for they are on this account the cheapest, and many of them can be had for the price of a poor man's dinner. It needs many a page to record even the names of the men and women who have become *somebody* and have done *something* just from reading some one worthy book which had fallen into their hands. Many believe that Franklin is the greatest American that has yet appeared, and he has said that "Cotton Mather's *essays to do good* gave me a turn of thinking which, perhaps, had an influence on some of the principal future events of my life."

As we become better acquainted with some of the *great* books in all departments of literature, we are surprised to find how few of them have been written by college men. This by no means belittles the good that may come from a *true* college course, but it does seem to emphasize that great books need some other environment for their growth than exclusive college courses. Perhaps the need is *solitude*, communion with nature, and frequent intercourse with the world's greatest and best in thought and feeling and action for the work. College-bred men are in a marked minority among the authors whose great books have been and are a potent force in shaping thought and conduct in the world. It is notable how few of these have anything commendatory to say about the influence which their college life had upon them and their accomplishments; many even of the text-books of schools and colleges have come from men whose powers were shaped by no school. How many text-books of medicine and law were prepared by physicians and lawyers whose knowledge was gleaned mainly from keen observation and long experience and deep thought!

It was no mere college education, but the sharpest home observation and strictest adherence to their instincts and their individuality that made forceful writers of Mark Twain, the Mississippi pilot; Bret Harte and William Dean Howells, the typesetters; James Whitcomb Riley, the itinerant sign-painter; Joel Chandler Harris and Eugene Field, the newspaper reporters; and Walt Whitman, the carpenter.

Of the four thousand and forty-three Americans with over twenty millions of dollars to their credit, only sixty-one had even a *high-school* course. Many among them, however, had high-class mentality and secured a comprehensive practical education. They have evidently been as alert to perceive the treasures hidden for them in the world of great books as they have been to perceive the treasuries hidden for them in their various enterprises. So we find that they have consulted the master spirits of books after their daily tasks were done, while myriads of those who scoff and sneer at them now because of their millions were feasting, frolicking, and dissipating. Among the highest types of American manhood to-day a large majority are the *new-rich* men. Whatever else may be said about them, all the world acknowledges that it is the parvenus in every land who do the largest part of the greatest work.

The larger our horizon becomes, the stronger is our conviction that the man himself is *mainly* the architect of his own fate; others may give an occasional lift, but it is almost entirely his own work. The college can do something for the *head-piece*, and it should also give something for the *heart-side* and the power to dare and to do; but all the external training in the world can never attain for the man what he can attain through his own individual efforts—provided he has lofty aims, firm resolutions, closely observes, and strictly adheres to all his best inborn powers. There was no college for David, Homer, Socrates, Plato, Confucius, Alexander, Cæsar, Dante, Luther, Shakespeare, Napoleon, Washington, Franklin, Goethe, Jesus, and tens of thousands of great or lesser men than these. They all marked out their own course, planned their own spiritual palaces; all the barbed-wire entanglements in the world did not retard their indomitable courage, self-reliance, and self-help.

Perhaps the chief use of all learning establishments, except those which have to do with what the Germans call *bread studies*, is to awaken the pupil's self-respect, which is the basis of all virtue, and to cultivate the powers that shall fit the pupil to consult for himself the *knowledge* and *power* books of the greatest and the wisest. They also can in these days do yeoman's service in giving the *bread studies* through which men shall be better able to do the world's work and thereby earn better wages.

XI

THOUGHTFULNESS

PRESIDENT WOLSEY, head of a great university, said that one of the chief purposes of the college is to cultivate the *power to think*. The college man who neglects to cultivate this valuable power until he enters upon his college career, instead of beginning it in the kindergarten and continuing it unremittingly throughout his entire preparatory course and daily living, will be liable to make sorry work of this part of his cultivation, or any other part, while he is in college.

The specialists who teach in colleges, and who are generally more interested in their specialties than in the science and art of education, may not be conscious of this, and yet the many educational wrecks that have come from colleges should long ago have brought this point most forcibly to their attention. Indeed, the power to think and the practice of thinking until it has become second nature, are so essential for success in any *worthy* career in life, that it is truer to say that one of the chief purposes of *life* itself is to cultivate and exercise the power to think, and keep right on thinking until close thinking shall become a habit. The power to think clearly, broadly, and successfully is not necessarily the prerogative of those only who have lived in a college environment, as the biographies of our own four thousand multi-millionaries in this country so cogently prove, for few of them ever darkened the doors of a college. Some among them may have been bereft of all the nobler sentiments for which Christianity and America stand, but they never could have piled up their millions in every department of activity without having thought so long and so hard that they ultimately acquired a habit of thinking that should put to shame myriads in every land who have had all the advantages of universities. The power to think, and to think in a masterly way, need not be confined to the professor's chair.

Any sphere of action which does not bring in to the worker an increase of thinking power is harmful, from university to street-sweeping. A machine is the only worker that can do its work well without thinking about it. All the successful men the world has ever known have been men who thought incessantly; they have been mainly self-educated in their extraordinary power to think; their success in all the various tasks which they set for themselves oftener resulted from their hard thought than from their hard work.

Defeat and failure have never overtaken the man whose head and hands were partners.

When we think without work or work without thought, we reach only half of what belong to us. A man should especially ween himself from this kind of halfness. We should be ashamed to find ourselves working without thought, as we should be ashamed to find ourselves idle in a world where there is always so much to be done and so little time allotted to each for accomplishing worthy work. The employees that are most valuable to their employers and are most valued by them are those always whose heads and hands are yoke-mates. When hands and head and heart are on the job, it is difficult to imagine what heights of success and service shall be attained. The farmer boy hoeing corn and digging potatoes will do better work in quantity and quality if he thinks about his work as hard as he hoes or digs.

There can be little danger of failure for any

young man who begins his life-work with the resolution that he will always give his best thought to even the most insignificant task that he assumes; and all the schools in the world cannot furnish him any advantage that can compare with this resolution steadily followed. Nor must the habit of thinking be exercised only upon work. We all have more leisure than work, and many a high-minded thinker has reminded us that a man is best to be judged, not by his profession, but by his leisure. Elihu Burritt acquired a knowledge of fifty languages during the years he earned his livelihood as a village blacksmith; he also found time for extensive reading as well as time for interest in social reforms, in the advancement of which he won the reputation of being one of the most powerful and persuasive orators of his day. All his stupendous acquirements were gained during the hours between his tasks which thousands of other village blacksmiths were accustomed to spend in gossip or in the tavern. Volumes could be filled with only *brief* accounts of the men and women throughout the ages who have made the world better for their living, just because they wisely and thoughtfully employed the leisure hours which their contemporaries trifled away. The shortest life may be long in noble thought and action, if we lose no time; and little of it is ever lost by those who thoughtfully employ their leisure.

Thoughtful men and women are always doubly valuable, no matter whether their work is what the world calls high-class or low-class. The streets are better swept by such a man, and the potatoes are better hoed; the floor is better scrubbed by such a woman, and the clothes are better washed. If our work does not afford us the chance to think while we are employed upon it, we owe it to ourselves and to humanity to toss it aside quickly. The lawyer, the physician, or any other professional man is no more a man in the sight of God and his country than the stone-mason who lays the foundations for their houses and raises the superstructures; and they are under no greater obligation to use their thinking powers than he is. The place we occupy in life is unimportant; the way we fill the place is everything; the stone-mason, Ben Jonson, built stone walls and houses by day, and at night built dramas and other poetry which have been surpassed only by his contemporary, Shakespeare.

Many of the greatest achievements known to history have been the work of men and women whose life-tasks were entirely different from the lines in which they became eminent; Shakespeare was an actor and one of the most successful business men of London, but he is known as the greatest poet the world has yet produced; George Eliot had charge for several years of her father's farm home, as well as the poultry and dairy, and won prizes for these at the country fair, but this did not prevent her from laying, during these seven years, the foundation which helped her to build herself into one of the greatest women known to history. Herschel's being a musician and Mary Somerville's having charge of her home and her children did not prevent both of them from doing marvelous work in astronomy. Audubon became a final authority on birds solely because while on his hunting-trips he thought more than the other hunters who accompanied him. One of the greatest merchants and capitalists in Boston began life selling handkerchiefs through the country. He became expert in flax products, and through this grew rich; he so studied kindred fibrous plants that his partners boasted that he had succeeded in marketing handkerchiefs made of twenty different fibrous plants. The most successful piano manufacturer now living was originally an employee of a steel mill that manufactured wire for making piano-strings. An every-day man gave careful thought to corn, and wrote an article for a magazine upon its value and upon the way it should be prepared for food; and this article was so worthy that it won for him a degree from a university.

Every waking moment of every man contains food for thought. If some live fuller lives every twenty-four hours than others live in a year, it is because they think faster and higher, wider and deeper, and because the discipline they get from this thought keeps them from wasting their time on trivial or worthless matter. A puddler in Youngstown, without education beyond the district school, began to think about the iron that was softened in the furnace before him, and asked questions of the older employees and the foreman; then he read upon the subject and became so capable in mining and iron manufacturing that when the Youngstown plant was sold to the great steel corporation he was the largest stockholder in forty-seven great companies manufacturing iron. Some men's hearts grow as hard as their gold while they are amassing riches; but his heart seems to have softened in proportion to the increase of his riches; his life is given to numberless good deeds, chief among which has been his endeavor to impress upon all workmen the necessity of letting both their heads and hearts assist their hands. Neither man nor boy, woman nor girl, need despair of doing great things and being great men and women, if they will constantly carry out this advice. He is really the best-educated man whose attention is primarily directed to his soul-growth, to his power of thinking, for feeling, and for noble action.

8

XII

INSTINCTS AND INDIVIDUALITY

"GOD has given us a full kit of watchmaker's tools" and if, after all the centuries of civilization, "we are doing *thinker's* work with them," something must be wrong with the educational methods. When God sent us here he packed us with all we need for high-class manhood—our *instincts* and our *individuality* especially well done up; but often in the unpacking by the schools we have been sadly marred; and these God-given endowments seem to have been frequently thrown upon the rubbish-pile. They seem to have dulled our instincts and to have despised our individuality, in order to make room for our acquirements.

Like all that emanates from God, instincts and individuality have been bestowed for a wise purpose; they are *indispensable* endowments if we shall become the kind of man God seems to have had in mind when he sent us here. What justification have the teachers of civilization for failing to perfect these powers? What right have the *little* men of the schools to drive them entirely out of their scheme of education?

John Ruskin complains in *Kings' Treasuries* that "Modern education for the most part signifies giving people the faculty of thinking wrong on every conceivable subject of importance to them." If this is even partly true, there is no pursuit to-day that demands from the man who is working in it more *presence of mind* and more *self-direction*, than the business of getting *real* education. Those who are to-day conducting what we are foolish enough to permit them to call *education* are often both blind and deaf to all that efficient education implies. To seek direction from them is like asking the road from a blind man. Many are also connected with the schools apparently as others are connected with hod-carrying and street-sweeping—to procure a livelihood. Often their highest conception of the work is *edge*ucation, to make sharp blades of the intellects for what they call "getting along in the world." Then many of the instructors in schools and colleges are merely specialists, mainly interested in their specialties, and using the class-room as a stepping-stone to their own purposes. Extreme specializing is narrowing—it does to the specialist what blinkers do to the horse's eyes. Excessive pursuit of single objects of thought atrophies many faculties, but *education* is the *complete* development and discipline of *all* the faculties.

Perhaps these are some of the causes why so many *original* and *thinking* men and women are so hostile to present-day schools, and accuse them of mainly being "places that polish pebbles and dim diamonds," and say so many other harsh and cutting things about them. Learning seems to be the *chief* occupation of those who profess to educate. Learning for its *own* sake plays a very *insignificant* part in the spiritual equipment of God's children; to a *true* education it seems at best only what the carpenter's kit is to the carpenter—a means to an end. Like all other lumber, its importance depends entirely upon what is built out of it. These original and thinking men and women have often said hard things of mere learning and of those who dole it out at so much a *unit*, because they believe that undue stress is laid upon it. They sometimes say that universities are not *educating* institutions, but merely *seats-of-learning;* and often they are very *narrow* seats, difficult for self-respecting people to stiffen their backs enough to sit upon. But it's the *study*, not the studies, that educates; studies make *learned* men, but not often *wise* men, such as *real* education always makes; not all learned heads are *sense*-boxes; the *very* learned man may be a very learned fool. The learned frequently put out their reasoning powers to make room for their learning; it requires ten pounds of *sense* to take care of one pound of learning.

Solomon made a book of proverbs, but a book of proverbs never made Solomon. Sense without learning is a thousand times superior to learning without sense; and in the stately edifice of life, school and college are only the basement walls; wisdom and learning are not necessary companions. The great things that have conduced to the betterment of the world have been done by men who have been loyal to their individuality and true to their instincts—never by the merely learned. Too often do we find these little learned men "displaying themselves offensively and ridiculously in the haunts of bearded men," and making the angels weep by their strutting and their swelling.

Knowing is only a *small* part of life; *doing* is nearly *all* of life; and the *best* done is done through *education*—the education which is the product of what is *inborn* as well as of what is *acquired;* the education which enables men and women to perceive and to cherish the *beautiful* in art, in literature, in morals and in nature. While true education busies itself with acquirements, it is even more concerned that the instincts and the individuality God appears to regard of supreme importance shall attain all that it is possible for them to have. These original and thinking men and women who say so many things in condemnation of *make-believe* education and mere learning boldly and lovingly acclaim the helps from true education—they remind us that it is soul-husbandry, spiritual perfection, torch and sword and shield, the *be-all* and the *end-all* of life, the fountain of all noble living, and the only real promoter of civilization. They claim that education of this sort simplifies life; facilitates self-conquest; intensifies individuality; unfolds and uplifts manhood; breeds habits of thinking, feeling, and doing; debestializes, emancipates, humbles, and civilizes; that it searches for truth, loves the beautiful, desires the good, and does the best.

We have no quarrel with the education that accomplishes all these, for it fosters the instincts and the individuality for which we are pleading. We have always believed that just this kind of education is the heritage of every American, and that the loss of such an education is the greatest calamity that can befall any one. All our life have we yearned that all might have this boon, and the best of our manhood years have been ceaseless labor and struggle to give "the weak and friendless sons of men" all of its advantages.

The test of any system of education is the kind of man it turns out. It is wisdom to measure the system by those it fails to educate rather than by those it does educate—by its tortoises rather than by its hares. The real educator is always vastly more concerned with the divinity than with the depravity of those intrusted to him; he believes firmly that the instincts and the individuality which God has given each of us are the priceless part of all our spiritual equipment—that anything we may acquire toward this end which fortifies these God-given treasures is cheap—even if bought by an entire life-service; that any acquirement that modifies these or destroys them is a triple curse and a dire menace to humanity, for individuality is the genius of Christianity and of America.

The system of education which makes light of the cultivation of the instincts, which seems to be the sole dependence of all conditions of men except the over-civilized, the system of education which is blinded to all that is implied in an educated individuality—these are the only systems with which we have any quarrel. Well-made, rather than well-filled heads are what is needed and should be demanded, without which it is impossible for any one of us to have the right conception of life, or to attain all that we were intended to be or to do. To guard and develop the instincts of the child, to preserve and fortify his individuality, is to give him sword and shield for the battle of life.

God intends each individual to be an individual, or this should not have been so deep-rooted in all; to be just like every one else is to be predestined for inferiority and failure. To do our duty consistently and steadfastly demands that all our God-like and God-given qualities shall first of all be educated. That best becomes a man which his individuality intended him to be, and those are always successful in making a life and a living who play the game of life with the cards their individuality gives them. God made a world for each separate man, and within that world he *must* live, if he will live effectually; we must first of all be ourselves, must see to it that whatever else is neglected the plants God has put into the individual shall be cultivated—the crop may not be large, but we are accountable for the cultivation, not for the crop. We must be ourselves, and do our own work.

There can be no greater wisdom and no greater service than that of helping another so that he may duly live in that special world which God has created for him. The most insignificant man can be complete if he is entirely true to his instincts and to his individual character. If we are incomplete, it is because we are living after some other method. We have all been stamped with individuality, but many seem to do their utmost to soak off the stamp. How different should the life of all the world be if each one only kept in his frame, and would not permit any one to try to make him part of, the picture for which his personality never intended him!

XIII

WOMEN

SOME women may be superficial in education and accomplishments, extravagant in tastes, conspicuous in apparel, something more than self-assured in bearing, devoted to trivialities, inclined to frequent public places. It is, nevertheless, not without cause that art has always shown the virtues in woman's dress, and that true literature teems with eloquent tributes and ideal pictures of true womanhood—from Homer's Andromache to Scott's Ellen Douglas, and farther. While Shakespeare had no heroes, all his women except Opehlia are heroines, even if Lady Macbeth, Regan, and Goneril are hideously wicked. In the moral world, women are what flowers and fruit are in the physical. "The soul's armor is never well set to the heart until woman's hand has braced it; and it is only when she braces it loosely that the honor of manhood fails."

Men will mainly be what women make them,

and there can never be *entirely free men* until there are *entirely free women* with no special privileges, but with all her rights. The wife makes the home, the mother makes the man, and she is the creator of joyous boyhood and heroic manhood; when women fulfil their divine mission, all reform societies will die, brutes will become men, and men shall be divine. There are unkind things said of her in the cheaper writings of to-day— perhaps because their authors have seen her only in boarding-houses, restaurants, theaters, dance-halls, and at card-parties; and the poor, degraded stage with its warped mirror shows her up to the ridicule of the cheaper brood. The greatest writings and the greatest dramas of all time have more than compensated for all this indignity, and we have only to read deep into the great literature to be disillusioned of any vulgar estimations of womanhood, and to understand the beauty and power of soul of every woman who is true to the royalty of womanhood.

There are few surer tests of a manly character than the estimation he has of women, and it is noteworthy that the men who stand highest in the esteem of both men and women are always men with worthy ideas of womanhood, and with praiseworthy ideals for their mothers, sisters, wives, and daughters. As men sink in self-respect and moral worth, their esteem of womanhood lowers. The women who become the theme for poets and philosophers and high-class playwrights are the women who have been bred mainly in the home. They seem without exception to abhor throngs, and only stern necessity can induce them to appear in them; the motherly, matronly, and filial graces appeal strongly to them—such as are portrayed in Cornelia, Portia, and Cordelia. They may yearn for society, but it is the best society—for the women whose beauty and sweetness and dignity and high accomplishments and grace make us understand the Greek mythology, and for the men who mold the time, who refresh our faith in heroism and virtue, who make Plato and Zeno and Shakespeare and all Shakespeare's gentlemen possible again."

If there is any inferiority in women, it is the result of environment and of lack of opportunity—never from lack of intelligence and other soul-powers. There is no sex in spiritual endowments, and woman seems entitled to all the rights of man—plus the right of protection. Ruskin says, "We are foolish without excuse in talking of the superiority of one sex over the other; each has attributes the other has not, each is completed by the other, and the happiness of both depends upon each seeking and receiving from the other what the other can alone give.

In speaking of the time when perfect manhood and perfect womanhood has come, Tennyson says in "The Princess":

Yet in the long years liker must they grow:
The man be more of woman, she of man;
He gain in sweetness and in moral height,
Nor lose the *wrestling* thews that throw the world;
She mental breadth, nor fail in childward care,
Nor lose the childlike in the larger mind.

Home is the true sphere for woman; her best work for humanity has always been done there, or has had its first impulse from within those four walls. It was home with all its duties that made the Roman matron Cornelia the type of the lofty woman of the world and the worthy mother. While it endowed her with the power to raise two sons as worthy as any known to history, who sacrificed their lives in defense of the Roman poor, it also endowed her with courage to say to the second of her sons when he was leaving her for the battle which brought his death, "My son, see that thou returnest with thy shield or on

OBSERVATION:—

it." Napoleon claimed that it was the women of France who caused the loss at Waterloo, not its men.

"Man's intellect is for speculation and invention, and his energy is for just war and just conquest; woman's intellect is for sweet ordering, arrangement, and decision; her energy is not for battle, but for rule." Apparently relying upon man's magnanimity not to resent her abdicating her home, woman's exigencies—and perhaps her ambitions—have forced her more and more during the past fifty years into man's domains of speculation and energy—perhaps into some war and some conquest. The ever-increasing demand for her in these man-realms which she has invaded or into which she has intruded herself is abundant evidence that she has creditably acquitted herself in the betterment of business, education, and literature, as well as in the numberless things which she has invented to add beauty and comfort to the home, and to remove much of the bitter drudgery from house and office, and to promote the health and happiness of millions. All these helps she has given, even if she has undoubtedly lost some of the graces which have always made so lovable the woman of whom Andromache, Portia, and Cordelia are but types,

124

EVERY MAN HIS OWN UNIVERSITY

Although matrimony and motherhood were the first conditions of women and only conditions that poets sing about and philosophers write about, and although these are still the conditions where she is doing her largest and noblest work in humanizing, yet her proper sphere is as man's, wherever she can live nobly and work nobly. How many myriads in this country alone are drudging or almost drudging in shops and offices to relieve the too stern pressure of pain or poverty from some one who is dear to them, yet are doing it unselfishly and uncomplainingly! A young woman lately told me that she had for several years been employed to interview women applicants for positions; that during these years she had interviewed scores of women daily, and had learned much of their private lives; that although the majority were working partly or entirely to maintain others, yet had she never heard one complaint of the sacrifices this service involved. Hundreds of other women, like George Eliot, Charlotte Brontë and Helen Hunt will long continue to bring pleasure and profit to millions through their writings.

It is women, too, whose inventions have not only lightened domestic work and brightened the home, but also have so far removed the modern

OBSERVATION:—

schoolroom from the little red schoolhouse of long ago; and it is women who have improved the books and the studies for children. They seem to have entered almost every activity outside of the home, and their finer powers of observation, aided by their innate love of the beautiful and the practicality they have learned while in service, seem mainly to have bettered conditions for wage-earners as well as for home and childhood. Think of the thousands upon thousands in this land whose work with the smaller children of the school could never be so well done by men! Think of the service daily rendered by women outside the home, and picture the confusion that would now arise if all these remained at home, even for one week!

As a class, women do not speak so well as men, but they excel him as a talker. In truth it is less difficult for them to talk little, than to talk well. Somebody has said that there is nothing a woman cannot endure if she can only talk. It is the woman who is ordained to teach talking to infancy. Those who see short distances see clearly, which probably accounts for woman's being able to see into and through character so much better than men. A man admires a woman who is worthy of admiration. As dignity is a man's quality.

loveliness is a woman's; her heart is love's favorite seat; women who are loyal to their womanhood can ever influence the gnarliest hearts. They go farther in love than men, but men go farther in friendship than women. Women mourn for the lost love, says Dr. Brinton, men mourn for the lost loved-one. A woman's love consoles; a man's friendship supports. What a real man most desires in a woman is womanhood. As every woman despises a womanish man, so every man despises a mannish woman.

Men are more sincere with the women of most culture, although mere brain-women never please them so much as heart-women. Men feel that it is the exceptional woman who should have exceptional rights; but they scorn women whose soul has shrunk into mere intellect, and a godless woman is a supreme horror to them. When to her womanly attributes she adds the lady's attributes of veracity, delicate honor, deference, and refinement, she becomes a high school of politeness for all who know her. "True women," says Charles Reade, "are not too high to use their arms, nor too low to cultivate their minds," but Hamerton believes that her greatest negative quality is, that she does not of her own force push forward intellectually; that she needs watchful masculine influence for this. It is claimed that single women are mainly best comforters, best sympathizers, best nurses, best companions.

Dean Swift says: "So many marriages prove unhappy because so many young women spend their time in making nets, not in making cages." Perhaps this is why they say that, in choosing a wife, the ear is a safer guide than the eye. The gifts a gentlewoman seeks are packed and locked up in a manly heart. Without a woman's love, a man's soul is without its garden. He is happiest in marriage who selects as his wife the woman he would have chosen as his bosom-companion, for a happy marriage demands a soul-mate as well as a house-mate or a yoke-mate. Spalding says that it is doubtful whether a woman should every marry who cannot sing and does not love poetry. The conceptions of a wife differ. When the Celt married, he put necklace and bracelets upon his wife; when the Teuton married, he gave his wife a horse, an ox, a spear, and a shield. A true wife delights both sense and soul; with her, a man unfolds a mine of gold. Like a good wine, the happiest marriages take years to attain perfection, and Hamerton says that marriage is a long, slow intergrowth, like that of two trees closely planted in a forest. The marriage of a deaf man and a blind woman is always happy; but this does not imply that conjugal happiness is attained only under these conditions. The greatest merit of many a man is his wife, but no real woman ever wears her husband as her appendage.

Maternity is the loveliest word in the language, and every worthy mother is an aristocrat. Mothers are the chief requisites of all educational systems, and the hand that rocks the cradle rules the world. The home has always been the best school in the world, and nothing else that is known to education can ever supersede it. The cradle is the first room in the school of life, and what is learned there lasts to the grave. Dearth of real mothers is responsible for dearth of real education. Each boy and each man is what his mother has made him, and every worthy mother rears her children to stand upon their own two feet, and to do without her.

While a thoughtful wife and mother is busied with the affairs of home, she is never done with her intellectual education, for she realizes early in her career that a mother loses half her influence with her children when she ceases to be their intellectual superior.

Women are far more observant of little things

than men, and the greatest among them have marvelous powers of observation. It is this power that made Mrs. Gladstone and Mrs. Disraeli the sturdy helpmates they were to their husbands in all their trying cares of government. It is said of Gladstone that it was not unusual for him to adjourn a Cabinet meeting through a desire "to consult with Catherine." Had there not been large power of observation, we should never have had the works of George Eliot, Charlotte Brontë, Jane Austin, Helen Hunt, and all the other notable women creators of fiction. Charlotte Cushman was the greatest actress America has ever produced because her observation was so close that not the smallest detail of the character she played escaped her or was neglected. The beautifying of Athens owes its inception to Aspasia rather than to Pericles.

XIV

MUSICAL CULTURE

OF all the arts, none is more difficult to define than music. No two persons seem to agree as to what it is, and a harsh sound to one is often sweet music to another. When music is controlled by those who use carefully their powers of observation, it will be vastly more useful to mankind. The need of music in the advancement of humanity it too apparent to admit of discussion. From the Greek instrument with one string down to the wonderful pipe-organ, music has been intensely attractive and marvelously helpful, and for the good of the human family.

No art or science needs more to be developed to-day than that of music. Its influence on soul and body has been noticed and advanced by some of the greatest thinkers of ancient and modern times, therefore it is not necessary to discuss the supreme need for real music to bring into harmony motives and movements for good. When we duly consider the subject of music, and ask where we shall find the great musicians who are to-day so much in demand, we feel that many so-called schools of music are often more misleading than instructive, and that they follow fashions that are far more unreasonable than the fashions of dress.

The art of music needs philosophic study, and it should be begun with a far better understanding of the many causes which contribute to its composition. The singing of birds is literally one of the most discordant expressions of sound. Indeed, the tones of the nightingale and the meadow-lark are only shrill whistles when they are considered with reference only to the tones of their voice, yet they furnish the ideal of some of the richest music to which the ear has ever listened, being one part of the delicate orchestra of nature. The lowing of the cow, the bellow of the bull, the bark of an angry dog echoing among the hills at eventide, combined with so many other different sounds and impressions, has become enticingly sweet to the pensive listener. The insect-choir of night has as much of the calming and refining influences as the bird-choir of the morning.

Real music requires not only that the tones

should be clear and resonant, but that they should be uttered amid harmonious surroundings. "Dixie" and "Yankee Doodle," sung with a banjo accompaniment on a lawn in the evening, surrounded by gay companions, may be the most delightful music, which will start the blood coursing or rest the disturbed mind, but it would not be called music if sung at a funeral. "I Know That My Redeemer Liveth" is glorious music when it is sung in a great cathedral, with echoes from its shadowy arches and the dim light of its stained-glass windows. But the same solo would be in awful discord with a ball-room jig.

Harmonious circumstances and appropriate environment are as essential for perfect effects in music as is the concord of sweet sounds. The foolish idea that music consists in screaming up to the highest C and growling down to the lowest B has misled many an amateur, and destroyed her helpfulness to a world that has far too much misery and far too little of the joy that comes from a sweet-voiced songster. The beginner in voice culture who attempts to wiggle her voice like a hired mourner, and with her tremulous effects sets the teeth of her audience on edge, has surely been misled into darkest delusion as to music, and will soon be lost amid the throng of vocal failures. Extremists are out of place anywhere, but the myriads of them in the musical world make humanity shudder.

What is needed in music to-day more than anything else is a standard of musical culture which shall demand careful discipline in all the influences that contribute to good music. True music is the music that always produces benign effects, the music that holds the attention of the auditor and permanently influences him to nobler thought, feeling, and action. Those large-hearted, artistic-souled men and women who are capable of interpreting into feeling what they have heard from voice or instrument must be the final court of appeal. A trapeze performance in acoustics is not music.

It has been frequently shown that music is potent in its effects upon the body as well as upon the soul. In 1901, a notable illustration of the power of music over disease was given at the Samaritan Hospital, connected with Temple University in Philadelphia, although the experiments were made under disadvantageous circumstances and environment. The patients were informed what the physicians were endeavoring to do, and the efforts of the first few months were wasted for the most part. Many of the patients who were placed under the influence of the music grew confident that they were going to be cured. While the recovery of some seemed miraculous, those who conducted the experiments felt that the healing might be largely due to the influence of the mind and not directly to the music. The matter was dropped for several months, until the patients were nearly all new cases. The doctors charged the nurses not to let the patients know for what cause the music was placed in the hospital. They eliminated also the personal influence of the nurses as well as the use of drugs at the time the music was produced. The experiment convinced those who conducted it that music has a powerful restorative effect even upon a person who is suffering from a combination of diseases. So many of the patients who recovered at that time from the influence of the music are alive and in good health to-day that common honesty disposes us to conclude that there is some undiscovered benefit in music which should be immediately investigated. This will never be attained by musical faddists or by selfish musicians who sing or perform for applause or money. Some plain, every day-man or woman will ultimately be the apostle of music for the people, and the experiments at Samaritan Hospital furnish only a suggestion of the resources of music which must soon be known to the world.

There was one patient in the hospital who had lost his memory through "softening of the brain." He lay most of the time unconscious, but occasionally talked irrationally upon all sorts of subjects. A quartet sang several pieces in his ward, but the nurses who sat upon each side of him noticed no effect whatever upon him until the quartet sang "My Old Kentucky Home." Then his eyes brightened and he began to hum the tune. Before they had finished the third verse, he asked the nurse about the singing, and requested the quartet to repeat the song. His intelligence seemed completely normal for a little while after the music ceased. He asked and answered questions clearly, but soon relapsed into his incoherent talk and listlessness.

When the man's lawyer heard of the effects upon the patient, he asked that the song might be sung while he was present, that he might then ask the patient about some very important papers of great value to the patient's family. As soon as the song was again sung by the quartet his intelligence returned. He informed the lawyer accurately as to the bank vault in which his box was locked, and told where he had left the keys in a private drawer of his desk.

Although the effect of the music was not permanent as to his case, many persons who know of it feel that some time music may be so applied as permanently to cure even such cases, if kept up for a sufficient length of time. Accidents to the skull, heart diseases, nervous exhaustion, and spinal ailments seem especially amenable to music. Two of the hospital cases of paralysis were permanently relieved by music. In one of these cases instrumental music seemed to produce a strong electric effect. While four violins were accompanied by an organ, the patient could use his feet and hands, but it was several weeks before he could walk without music. In the other case, vocal music put an insomnia patient to sleep, but after sleeping through the program, the patient was better; after a few trials he returned home.

Some of the hundred cases experimented upon were complete failures. But those conducting the experiments were convinced that the failure was attributable to the fact that they were unable to find the right kind of music. In the use of religious selections, "Pleyel's Hymn" made the patients of every ward worse; but "The Dead

March" from Saul was soothing to typhoid patients. When this march was rendered softly, the nurses discovered that two cases had been so susceptible to the influences of the music that the physicians omitted the usual treatment and the patients recovered sooner than some other patients who had the disease in a less dangerous form.

Children were helped by a different class of music from that used with adults, and difference in sex also was noted. Mothers who sing to their children may become the best investigators as to the power of vocal music on the healthy development of childhood.

In the Baptist Temple, Philadelphia, several hymns were once forcefully rendered by the great chorus of the church to a congregation of three thousand people. At the close, slips of paper were passed to the worshipers, and they were asked to write upon the paper what thoughts the music had suggested to them. While there was nothing in the anthems suggestive of youth, and the burden of the stanzas seemed to divert from childhood, yet more than half of the two thousand slips returned attested that the hearer had been reminded of his schooldays and of the games of childhood; these slips were collected before the congregation had time to confer. It shows that the music was not in accord with the words, and that it had greater power upon the mind than the words had. It proves that, to produce its highest effects, sacred music must harmonize with the meaning of the words and with the environment. It also shows that the purpose for which one sings is an important factor—random vociferations or a display of vocal gymnastics even of the most cultured kind is both inartistic and unmusical.

These pages have been written to suggest that music is still with the common people; that the future blessings which mankind shall derive from musical art and science are probably dependent upon some observant person who is free from the trammels of misguided and misdirected culture, and who may come to it with an independent genius, and handle the subject in the light of every-day common-sense.

XV

ORATORY

ORATORY has always been a potent influence for good. The printing-press with its newspapers and magazines and tens of thousands of books has done much during the past fifty years to draw attention away from oratory. The printing-press is a huge blessing, and has greatly advanced during these years that oratory has declined in public esteem or public attention. But we are learning that there is yet something in the *living* man, in his voice and his manner and his mesmeric force, which cannot be expressed through the cold lead of type. Hence the need for orators, both men and women, has been steadily increasing during the past few years, until there seems to be a pressing demand for the restoration of the science and the art of oratory.

The country lad or the hard-working laborer or mechanic who thinks that public speaking is beyond his reach has done himself a wrong.

It was such as they who oftener than can be told have become some of the greatest orators of history. Men who afterward became great as effective debaters made their first addresses to the cows in the pasture, to the pigs in pens, to the birds in trees, and to the dog and the cat upon the hearth. They often drew lessons concerning the effects of their addresses from the actions of the animal auditors which heard their talk, and were attracted or repulsed by what they heard and saw.

There is a mystery about public speaking. After years of study and application, some men cannot accomplish as much by their addresses as some uncultured laborer can do with his very first attempt. Some have imperfectly called this power "personal magnetism." While this is mainly born with men and women—as the power of the true poet and the true teacher—yet it can be cultivated to a surprising degree. The schools of elocution so often seem to fail to recognize the wide gulf that exists between elocution and oratory. The former is an art which deals primarily with enunciation, pronunciation, and gesture; the work of the later science is persuasive— it has to do mainly with influencing the head and the heart.

There is a law of oratory which does not seem

to be understood or recognized by elocution teachers. The plow-boy in a debating society of the country school may feel that natural law, like Daniel Webster, without being conscious that he is following it. But there is a danger of losing this great natural power through injurious cultivation. The powerful speaker is consciously or unconsciously observant at all times of his audience, and he naturally adopts the tones, the gesture, and the language which attract the most attention and leave the most potent influence upon the audience. That is the law of all oratory, whether it applies to the domestic animals, to conversation with our fellows, to debates or addresses, lectures, speeches, sermons, or arguments. Where the orator has not been misdirected or misled by some superficial teacher of elocution, his aim will be first "to win the favorable attention of his audience" and then to strongly impress them with his opening sentence, his appearance, his manners, and his subject. His reputation will have also very much to do with winning this favorable impression at first. The words of the speaker either drive away or attract, and the speaker endeavors at the outset to command the attention of the hearers, whether they be dogs or congregation.

EVERY MAN HIS OWN UNIVERSITY

The beginner in oratory who is true to his instincts strives to adopt the methods which he feels will favorably impress those for whom he has a message. In his oration at the funeral of Julius Cæsar, Mark Anthony disarmed the enemies of Cæsar and of himself by opening his oration with, "Friends, Romans, countrymen, lend me your ears. I come to bury Cæsar, not to *praise* him." Almost any man or woman can become an orator of power by keeping himself or herself natural while talking.

The second condition of a successful oration is the statements of the important facts or truths. Cicero, the elder Pitt, and Edward Everett held strictly to the statement of all the facts at the outset of their speech. Facts and truths are the most important things in all kinds of oratory; as they are the most difficult to handle, the audience is more likely to listen to them at the opening of the talk, and they must be placed before the hearers clearly and emphatically, before the speaker enters upon the next division of his address.

The third condition of a successful address is the argument, or reasoning which is used to prove the conclusion he wishes his hearers to reach. It is here that logic has its special place; it is at this vital point that many political speakers fail to convince the men they address. After he has thus reasoned, the natural orator makes his appeal, which is the *chief purpose* of all true oratory. It is here where the orator becomes vehement, here where he shows all the ornament of his talk in appropriate figures of speech. The most effective orators are always those whose hearts are in strong sympathy with humanity, and whose sympathies are always aroused to plead for men. This is the condition that accounts for the eloquence—the power to arouse hearers—which characterizes men like Logan, the American Indian, and which characterizes many of the religious enthusiasts like Peter the Hermit, who have surprised the world and often moved them to mighty deeds.

So long as our government depends upon the votes of the people, just so long must there be a stirring need of men and women orators to teach the principles of government and to keep open to the light of truth the consciences of the thousands and millions whose votes will decide the welfare or the misfortune of our nation. As the speaker must adapt himself and his message to all kinds of people, it is difficult to advise any one in certain terms how to accomplish this. It is another instance of the necessity of cultivating the daily habit of observation, and of being always loyal to our instincts.

While schools and colleges have their uses, they are by no means a necessity for those who will accomplish great things through their oratory. Many a man laden with a wealth of college accomplishment has been an utter failure on the platform. Where reading-matter is as abundant and as cheap as it is in America, the poor boy at work upon the farm or in the factory, with no time but his evenings for study, may get the essentials of education, and by observing those who speak may give himself forms of oratorical expression that will enable him to outshine those with scholarship who have been led into fads.

We must be impressed with a high sense of duty in becoming an orator of any class; we must feel that it is our calling to adhere to the truth always and in all things, to warn our hearers of dangers, and to encourage the good and help those who are struggling to be so. We must have a passion for oratory which shall impel us to vigorous thought and eloquent expression. The greatest oratory is that which is most persuasive. It is not so fully in what an orator says or the vehemence with which he says it that counts, but the practical good that results from it. Many an oration has been elegant enough from its choice diction and labored phraseology, yet it has fallen flat upon the audience.

When a man has been worked into natural passion over his theme, his words will strike root and inspire his hearers into similar passion. It is wonderful how true are our instincts in detecting what comes from the heart and that which is mere words. The greatest orators have been those who have not learned "by rote" what they have spoken. When Lincoln broke away in his celebrated Cooper Institute address, and pictured the word freedom written by the Lord across the skies in rainbow hues, the hearts of his audience stopped beating for the instant. It is foolhardy for any one to presume to speak with no preparation, for those who wish to give themselves to oratory should carefully study the great debaters, learn how they expressed themselves, and then accumulate important truths and facts concerning their subject. But we must not forget that too much study as to nicety of expression may lose something of the mountainous effects of what we wish to state.

When an orator *feels* his subject, his soul overflows with a thrill indescribable, which is known only to those who have felt it. Genius is lifted free for the moment to fly at will to the mountain heights, and finds supreme delight therein. Everything that is food for the mind is helpful to the orator, whether it come from school or work. But it is an attainment which can be reached by the every-day plain man employed in any every-day occupation. Demosthenes, the greatest orator the world has yet known, found his School of Oratory along the shore talking to the waves. John B. Gough and Henry Clay and both the elder and the younger Pitt gained all their powers by means as humble. The mere study of grammar has never yet made a correct speaker; the mere study of rhetoric has never yet made a correct and powerful writer; and the study of elocution cannot make an orator. Grammar, rhetoric, and elocution may teach him only the laws which govern speech, writing, oratory, and leave him ignorant of the best methods of execution.

During the last hundred years the leading orators of Congress have mainly come from among the humble and the poor, and all the learning they had of their art was got in the schoolhouse, the shop, the fields, and the University of Hard Knocks. It is a calling that seems to be open to every man and woman of fair talent. If you desire to become a platform orator, read the lives of successful orators, and apply to yourself the means which helped them to distinction. But be viligant not to lose your own individuality, and never strive to be any one but yourself. In no place more than upon the platform does *sham* mean *shame*; nothing is more transparent.

XVI

SELF-HELP

ALTHOUGH Samuel Smiles's "Self-Help" is the first and perhaps the best of the many inspirational books that have been written of late years, it is by far the most serviceable of all to any one who wishes and intends to stand squarely on his own feet and to fight his own battle of life from start to finish. That book is attractive because it is anecdotal of life and character, and because of the interest that all men feel in those who have achieved great things through their own labors, their trials, and their struggles. It abounds with references to men who were forced to be self-helpful, who were born lowly enough, but died among God's gentlemen, and often among the aristocracy of the land, through sheer force of character, labor, and determination. They have left their "footprints on the sands of time" mainly because they were *self-reliant* and *self-helpful*.

The aids to the royal life are all within, and no

life is worthless unless its owner wills it; the fountain of all good is within, and it will bubble up, if we dig.

Doctor Holland used to say that there is a super-abundance of inspiration in America, but a lamentable dearth of perspiration. Aspiration plus perspiration carries men to dizzy heights of success; aspiration minus perspiration often lands them in the gutter.

Self-help is not selfishness. The duty of helping oneself in the highest sense always involves the duty of helping others. The self-helpful are not always the men who have achieved greatest success in what vulgarians call success. That man's life is a success which has attained the end for which he started out—the greatest failure may sometimes be the hugest success through the discipline it has afforded. They tell us that men never fail who die in a worthy cause; that it is nobler to have failed in a noble cause than to have won in a low one; that it is not failure, but low aim, that is wicked. God sows the seed and starts us all out with about the same quantity and the same quality; whether the crop shall be abundant depends upon the environment in which we grow and the way we take care of the field.

The supreme end of each man's life is to take

individual care of his own garden. When this is neglected his life is wasted, and there is no immorality that is comparable to the immorality of a wasted life—and every life is wasted unless its owner has made it yield its full capacity. If it is only a ten-bushel-an-acre field, he has done worthy work who has reaped ten bushels from an acre; if it is a seventy-bushel-an-acre field it is dishonorable to have reaped sixty-nine bushels from an acre. God gives us the chance; the improvement of it we give ourselves.

The spirit of self-help is the root of all genuine growth. Help from the outside may be convenient, but it enfeebles; all self-help invigorates. The self-helper must be self-reliant; the measure of his self-help is always proportioned to the measure of his self-reliance. The self-reliant does not consider himself as the creature of circumstances, but the architect of them. "All that Adam had, all that Cæsar could, we have had and can." The self-reliant and the self-helpful are the minority; the majority are forever looking toward and relying upon some government or some institution to do for them what they should only do for themselves. A real man wants no protection; so long as his human powers are left to him, he asks nothing more than the freedom to win his own battles. The best any government or any institution can do for men is to leave them as free as possible from either guidance or help, so that they may best develop and improve themselves. As it has been during the centuries, we put too much faith in government and other institutions, and too little in ourselves.

Men who count for something do not wait for opportunities from any source—they help themselves to their opportunities. They can win who believe they can, and the strong-hearted always ultimately achieve success. A nation is worth just what the individuals of that nation are worth, and the highest philanthropy and patriotism does not wholly consist in aiding institutions and enacting laws—especially the laws which teach men to lean—but they rather consist in helping men to improve themselves through their own self-help. There is no aid comparable to the aid that is given a man to help himself—we may stand him upon his feet, but remaining upon them should be his own task. He is a magnificent somebody who steadfastly refuses to hang upon others; and nothing brings the blush sooner to the true-hearted man, than to feel that he has been unnecessarily helped to anything by men or by governments. There is no man who rides through life so well as the man who has learned to ride by being set upon the bare-backed horse called self-dependence.

Paradise was not meant for cowards; self-reliance and self-help is the manliness of the soul.

The solid foundations of all liberty rest upon individual character, and individual character is the only sure guaranty for social security and national progress. Whatever crushes individuality is despotism, no matter by what other name you call it. The gods are always on the side of the man who relies on himself and helps himself; men's arms are long enough to reach stars, if they will only stretch them. It is so contrary to the spirit of our nation to be anything but self-helpful. "The flag of freedom cannot long float over a nation of deadheads; only those who determine to pay their way from cradle to grave have a right to make the journey." Schiller says that the kind of education that perfects the human race is action, conduct, self-culture, self-control. It has been said that the individual is perfected far more by work than by reading, by action more than by study, by character more than by biography; these are courses that are given by the University of Life more completely than in all other institutions known to men.

OBSERVATION:—

The great men of science, literature, art, action—those apostles of great thoughts and lords of the great heart—belong to no special rank. They come from colleges, workshops, farms, from poor men's huts and rich men's mansions; but they all began with reliance upon themselves, and with an instinctive feeling that they must help themselves solely in climbing to the work or the station which they had assigned to themselves. Many of God's greatest apostles of thought and feeling and action have come from the humblest stations, but the most insuperable difficulties have not long been obstacles to them. These greatest of difficulties are true men's greatest helpers— they stimulate powers that might have lain dormant all through life, but often have readily yielded to the stout and reliant heart. There is no greater blessing in the world than poverty which is allied to self-reliance and the spirit of self-help. "Poverty is the northwind which lashes men into vikings." Lord Bacon says that men believe too great things of riches, and too little of indomitable perseverance.

Every nation that has a history has a long list of men who began life in the humblest stations, yet rose to high station in honor and service. No inheritance and environments can do for a man what he can do for himself. Cook, the navigator, Brindley, the engineer, and Burns, the poet, are three men who began life as day laborers; the most poetic of clergymen, Jeremy Taylor; the inventor of the spinning-jenny and founder of cotton manufacture, Sir Richard Arkwright; the greatest of landscape painters, Turner, and that most distinguished Chief-justice Tenterden were barbers. Ben Jonson, the poet; Telford, the engineer; Hugh Miller, the geologist; Cunningham, the sculptor, were English stone-masons. Inigo Jones, the architect; Hunter, the physiologist; Romney and Poie, the painters; Gibson, the sculptor; Fox, the statesman; Wilson, the ornithologist; Livingstone, the missionary—started life as weavers. Admiral Sir Cloudesly Shovel; Bloomfield, the poet; Carey, the missionary—were shoemakers. Bunyan, was a tinker; Herschel, a musician; Lincoln, a rail-splitter; Faraday, a bookbinder; Stephenson, the inventor of the locomotive, a stoker; Watt, the discoverer of steampower, a watchmaker; Franklin, a printer; President Johnson, a tailor; President Garfield, an employee on a canal-boat; Louisa Alcott, both housemaid and laundress; James Whitcomb Riley, an itinerant sign-painter; Thoreau, a man-of-all-work for Emerson; the poets, Keats and Drake, as well as Sir Humphry Davy, were druggists.

Benjamin Thompson was a humble New Hampshire schoolmaster whose industry, perseverance, and integrity, coupled to his genius and a truly benevolent spirit, ultimately made him the companion of kings and philosophers, Count Rumford of the Holy Roman Empire. He declined to participate in the Revolution, and was compelled to flee from his home in Rumford, now Concord (New Hampshire), leaving behind his mother, wife, and friends; but this persecution by his countrymen led to his greatness. In the spring of 1776 General Howe sent him to England with important despatches for the Ministry. At once the English government appreciated his worth and scientific men sought his acquaintance. In less than four years after he landed in England he became Under-Secretary of State. In 1788, he left England with letters to the Elector of Bavaria, who immediately offered him honorable employment which the English government permitted him to accept after he had been knighted by the king.

In Bavaria he became lieutenant-general, commander-in-chief of staff, minister of war, member of the council of state, knight of Poland, member of the academy of science in three cities, commander-in-chief of the general staff, superinten-dent of police of Bavaria, and chief of the regency during the sovereign's compulsory absence in 1798. During his ten years' service he made great civil and military reforms and produced such salutary changes in the condition of the people that they erected a monument in his honor in the pleasure-grounds of Munich, which he had made for them. When Munich was at-tacked by an Austrian army in 1796, he conducted the defense so successfully that he was accorded the highest praise throughout Europe. The Bavarian monarch showed his appreciation by making him a count; he chose the title of Count Rumford as an honor to the birthplace of his wife and child. He ended his days at Paris in literary and scientific studies and in the society of the most learned men of Europe.

The Rumford professorship at Harvard was very liberally endowed by him, and he gave five thousand dollars to the American Academy of Arts and Sciences in 1796.

XVII

SOME ADVICE TO YOUNG MEN

A LIFE is divine when duty is a joy. The best work we ever do is the work we get pleasure from doing, and the work we are likeliest to enjoy most is the work we are best fitted to do with our talent. There is nothing in the world except marriage that we should be slower in taking upon ourselves than our life-work; therefore, think much, read much, inquire much before you assume any life career.

When you have once decided what is best fitted for you, pursue it ceaselessly and courageously, no matter how far distant it may be, how arduous the labor attending it, or how difficult the ascent. The greater the difficulty surmounted, the more you will value your achievement and the greater power you will have for keeping on with your work after you have reached your goal. Do your utmost to find a friend who is older than you, and consult him freely, and give every man your ear, for the humblest in station and those with the most meager acquirements in other matters may see some few things more clearly than other men, and may be well stored with what you most require. Take each man's advice, but act according to your own judgment. Teachers should be the best advisers of those about to enter upon their life-work, and no service of the schoolmaster or professor can ever be more helpful to the young intrusted to him than that of helping them to choose a career.

The best work real teachers do for their pupils is by no means the teaching of a few minor branches—it is almost always the work he is not paid for, and which nobody outside of those who realize what real education is, seems ever to consider. It is sympathy for their students, getting them to understand the great things that are involved in the process of getting an education, making them realize that true education means growth of all our spiritual faculties—head and heart and will, and that what we get from textbooks is the very least part of an education. It is helping them to understand that knowledge got from books and from schoolmasters is always a menace to a man whose spiritual faculties of head, heart, and will have not been thoroughly disciplined. It is wise counsel in choosing a life career. Instead of looking upon this side of the work as divine, instead of being wise counselors and friendly guides during this great transitional stage from youth to manhood, teachers can be far more interested in their individual concerns or in what they call "research-work"—the research-work may give some temporary glory to themselves, and give some little advertisement to the institutions that employ them; but the supreme duty they owe to their students, to God, and to humanity is to do their utmost to make full men, and worthy and successful men, out of the youths whose education they have taken upon themselves. No traitor is such a traitor to his country and to the whole world as the man who is unfaithful to this sacred trust. Once again, find some sincere and prudent elder counselor, and turn to him in all your difficulties.

Get advice as to the best books to read—a good book is the best of counselors, for it is the best of some good man; and it is a patient counselor whom we may continually consult upon the same subject as often as we wish. But waste no time, especially at the opening of your career, upon books which have no message for your manhood and no helpfulness in the work you shall assume for life. When you have once taken up a book as your counselor, don't put it aside until it has been thoroughly digested and assimilated. One book read is worth a hundred books peeped through; and of all the dilettantes, a literary dilettante is the most contemptible. Bacon says, "Some books are to be tasted, others to be swallowed, some few to be chewed and digested." But it is only the books that are to be chewed and digested that we can afford to peruse at the outset in our career; the literary pleasure—gardens—may come later in life.

Do your utmost to understand poetic expression, for the poets are the greatest teachers in the world as well as the greatest of all legislators. It is they who teach the great in conduct and the pure in thought. Without education that shall enable us to take them as our friends, life bears upon it the stamp of death. The great poets are now the only truth-tellers left to God. They are free, and they make their lovers free; the great poet is nature's masterpiece. At the touch of his imagination words blossom into beauty. A true poet is the most precious gift to a nation, for he feels keenest the glorious duty of serving truth; he cannot strive for despotism of any kind, for it is still the instinct of all great spirits to be free. More than other authors, the poets make us self-forgetful, make life and the whole human race nobler in our eyes; all things are friendly and sacred to them, all days holy, all good men divine.

There is very little worthy work nowadays that does not need some schooling that it may be well done. If you have an opportunity to give your-self this help, don't neglect it. Carefully select the courses that will be most helpful to you in your career, and don't be side-tracked by any of what we sentimentalists term "culture studies." There's nothing better in the world than culture study, if we can afford it and have time for it. But there is not a greater or more wicked waste of valuable time than the time spent upon what some sentimentalists term culture study.

When you have once taken up the studies you have decided upon, keep steadily to your course and shun diversions. Recreations are as essential to the student who intends to do high-class work as food is to the body; but diversions disqualify him for earnest work, and may breed a habit of halfness that shall bring his failure. Don't be foolish and hope to be great in many lines. Who sips of many arts drinks none. In every vocation to-day competition is so keen that the man who

EVERY MAN HIS OWN UNIVERSITY

will succeed must be content to be supreme in one thing alone.

Halfness weakens all our spiritual powers, and thoroughness is the *central* passion of all worthy characters.

It is nobler to be confined to one calling, and to excel in that, than to dabble in forty. There is some odor about a dabbler that makes him especially offensive to all clean high-class men and women. But when we have formed the habit of doing carelessly other tasks than our life-work, we shall soon get into the way of doing carelessly the work of our chosen calling. There is nothing that gives us greater assurance that our life-work will be thoroughly done than to habituate ourselves to do the slightest task completely. Sing the last note fully, make the last letter of your name complete. Eat the last morsel deliberately. In a real man's life there are no trifles. Whatever is worth doing by him is worth doing well. The many-sided Edward Everett attributed his being able to do so many things well to his early habit of doing even the least thing thoroughly. He used to say that he prided himself upon the way he tied up the smallest paper parcel.

Although schools may be very helpful, don't forget to emphasize again that they are merely

helpers. The man is somebody only when the
fight is won within himself. Without the schools
men have often reached the pinnacles of success,
through their own individual earnestness and
energy. Schools make wise men wiser, but they
may make fools greater fools than ever. If
colleges have fallen somewhat into disrepute, it is
largely due to the fact that we may have sent
more fools than wise men to college. Many a man
has been the better for being too poor to attend
school, like Franklin, Lincoln, Peter Cooper, and
ten thousand other Americans. Their thirst for
what books had to give them forced them to
work harder and to deny themselves all the enjoy-
ments that so vulgarize yet so charm the cheaper
brood.

All that is won by sacrifice and downright hard
work is priceless, and many noble men and
women who have risen to high honor and station
owe their place and power solely to this. Be
always mindful that power is the only safe foundation for reputation. Thoughtful Americans are
not concerning themselves about who your ancestors were, and whether or not they were graduated from some college. Like Doctor Holmes, they
feel that old families and old trees generally have
their best parts underground, and that the only

progressive is the man who is bigger in thought and feeling and accomplishment than his father was. They believe that it is unimportant where you buy your educational tools, if you are only doing good work with them.

There is only one *true aristocracy in America*—those with more spiritual power and individual accomplishment than the rest of men.

Emerson says that "all the winds that move the vanes of universities blow from antiquity," and this is responsible for many foolish words and many fool acts of schoolmen which are so often misleading the unsuspecting public.

Nothing is more foolish than the idea that any schooling is worthless which is obtained in schools after the regular school hours; and more than one attempt has been made to enact laws which shall hinder from practice physicians and lawyers who have been obliged to get their knowledge through channels other than the conventional. The victory of the general does not depend upon the place where he got his military training or the time of the day when he studied. Oliver Cromwell, the greatest general of his day, was a farmer until his fortieth year, when he entered the army of the Parliament against Charles I. The only question that concerns the nation that puts a general at the head of its forces is, has he the powers that shall make us victorious?

Men in distress don't ask for the pedigree of the life-saver, nor do they stop to inquire when he graduated. Don't be frightened off by sticklers for what is customary. Knowledge is the right of the poorest boy and girl in America, and it can be had by the humblest in the land. Be convinced of this and enter the race. The world steps aside and lets the man pass who knows where he is going; all the world will shout to clear the track when they see a determined giant is coming. In choosing your career, don't be limited to the old professions. There are to-day many more occupations calling for the highest skill and offering the highest inducements than there were twenty years ago, and these positions are steadily increasing. Many occupations which were recently regarded almost as menial have risen almost to professions—cooking, agriculture, decorative art, forestry, nursing, sanitation, designing apparel, and countless others; and the men and women qualified for these are surer of better positions than formerly, and far better rewards.

But the youth who is imbued with the determination to *be* right and to *do* right must never lose sight of this truth—that life is vastly more than place and meat and raiment. Living for self is suicide; men that are men get far greater enjoyment and far greater reward from making life a blessing for those who come their way than they get from all other things combined. No man lives so truly for himself as he who lives for other people, and one of the chiefest purposes of education is that it gives larger views of life and adds greater power to serve humanity. The man who is really in earnest to make his life count is studiously observant. Each day and each place multiplies his means of happiness for himself and others.

THE END

RECENT BIOGRAPHIES
AND REMINISCENCES

A DIPLOMAT'S WIFE IN MEXICO
BY EDITH O'SHAUGHNESSY
Intimate personal experiences at Mexico City and Vera Cruz during those dramatic months in 1913 and 1914, when Nelson O'Shaughnessy was American Chargé d'Affaires. Illustrated. Octavo

THE SUNNY SIDE OF DIPLOMATIC LIFE
BY MADAME DE HEGERMANN-LINDENCRONE
As the wife of a Danish diplomat she has many gossipy bits to relate of life in Washington, Rome, Denmark, Paris and Berlin. Illustrated. Octavo

IN THE COURTS OF MEMORY
BY MADAME DE HEGERMANN-LINDENCRONE
An American woman with eyes and ears would have had much to see and hear at the court of Napoleon III. It is exactly this fascinating story that is told in this book. Illustrated. Octavo

THE STORY OF A PIONEER
By ANNA HOWARD SHAW; with the collaboration of Elizabeth Jordan
Frontierswoman, school-teacher, preacher, lecturer, minister, physician, worker among the poor — and President of the National American Woman's Suffrage Association—Dr. Anna Shaw tells her life history in an astonishing human document. Illustrated. Crown 8vo

MARK TWAIN: A Biography
By ALBERT BIGELOW PAINE
The personal and literary life of Samuel Langhorne Clemens. Three volumes in a box. Octavo

HARPER & BROTHERS
NEW YORK   ESTABLISHED 1817   LONDON

BOOKS ON ELECTRICITY

A-B-C OF ELECTRICITY
BY WILLIAM H. MEADOWCROFT

Simple and clear explanations of the various ways by which electricity is obtained and applied.

HARPER'S BEGINNING ELECTRICITY
BY DON CAMERON SHAFER

A secondary book containing general explanations and their applications, with instructions in making simple electrical appliances.

HARPER'S EVERY-DAY ELECTRICITY
BY DON CAMERON SHAFER

How to use electricity with explanations of practical ways and means for electrical experiments and home construction.

HARPER'S ELECTRICITY BOOK
BY JOSEPH H. ADAMS

A comprehensive, practical book showing how those who are interested in electricity can carry their experiments further and gain working results for themselves in a wide variety of fields.

HARPER'S HOW TO UNDERSTAND ELECTRICAL WORK
BY WILLIAM H. ONKEN, JR. and JOSEPH B. BAKER

A general guide to a knowledge of the great commercial applications of electricity with which we are surrounded—clean-cut explanations of the modern uses of electricity in transportation, manufacturing, farming, mining, the household, etc. A book necessary to a knowledge of the work of modern life.

HARPER & BROTHERS
NEW YORK   ESTABLISHED 1817   LONDON

37202067R00120

Made in the USA
Lexington, KY
21 November 2014